MINA

THE FREE

The story of a rescued friend...
by Jeremy Duplaquet and Lauran Doverspike
2014

This book is dedicated to
Charli, Caleb, & Sammy

With all my love,
Aunt Laura

...with special thanks to Mina for her great
performances!

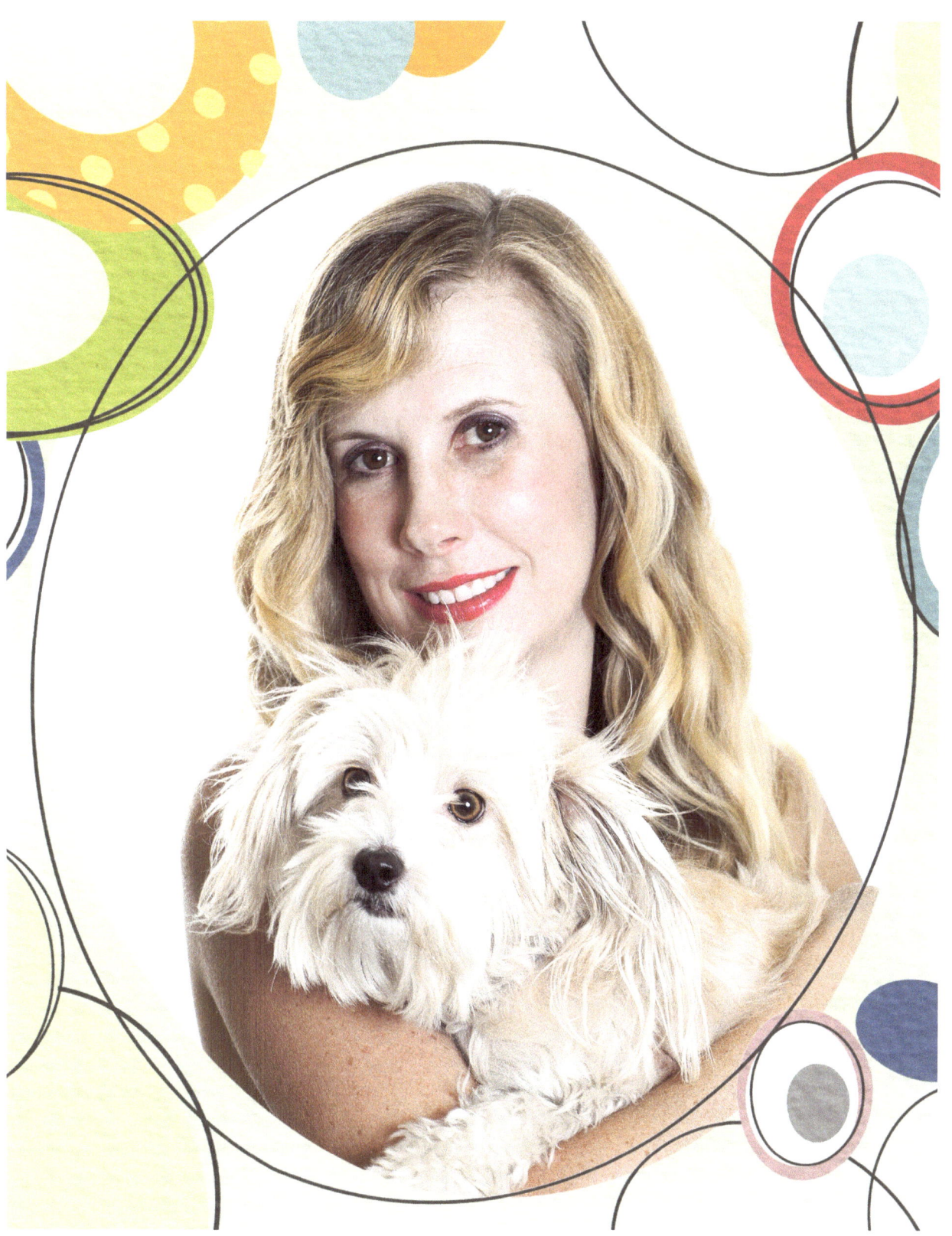

ONCE UPON A TIME...
IN A LAND
FAR, FAR AWAY...

well, actually at the present time,
in a land much like your own,
lives a magnificent little creature.

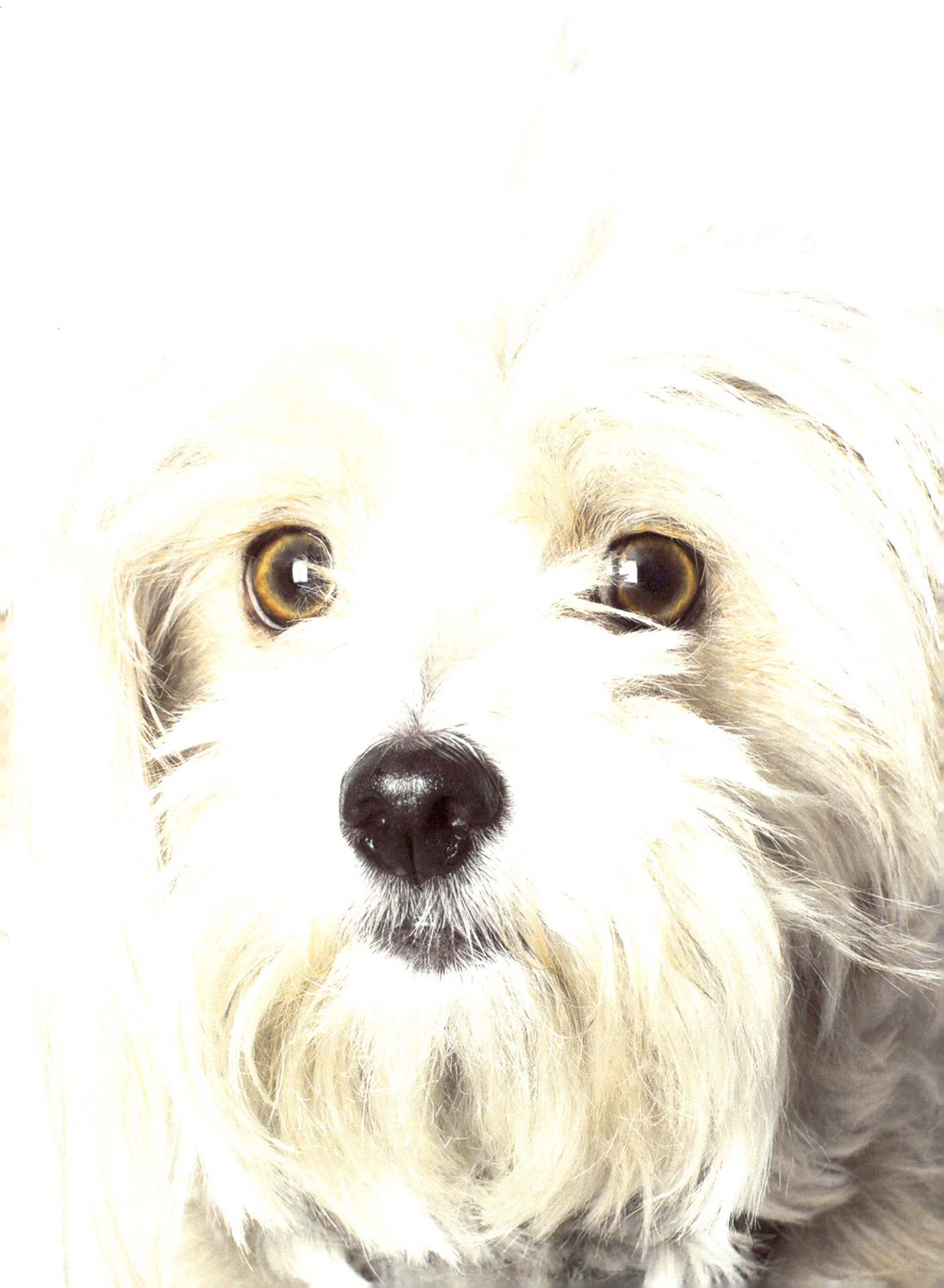

"Nice to meet you!

My name is Mina!

Let me tell you my story!"

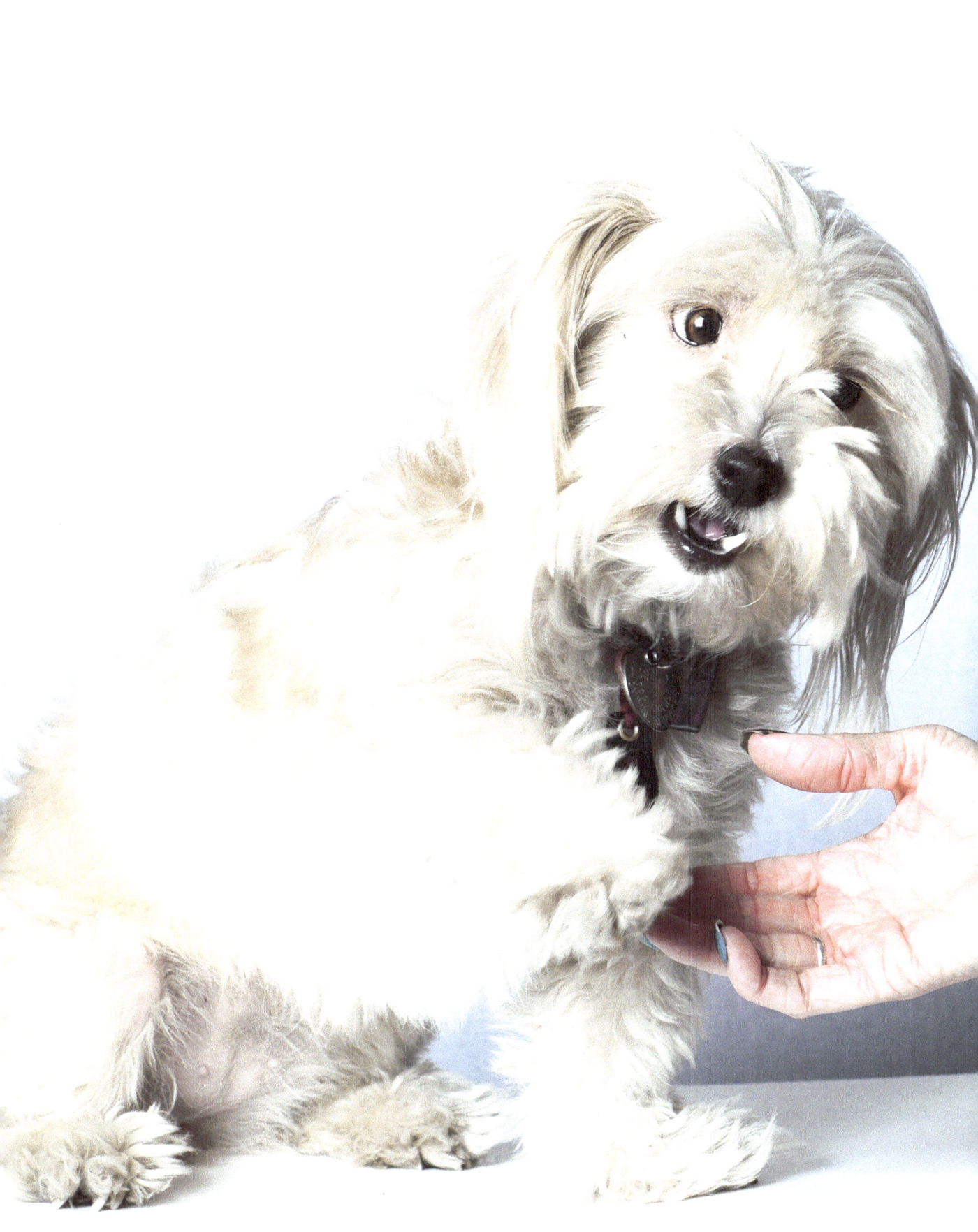

Years ago, in my life, I suffered a hurtful battle.

We all need to see the bad to know the good.

I was abandoned by my first family into a high-kill

shelter in a bad area of Los Angeles.

I didn't understand why they would just leave me

behind, so I stopped eating and shook so hard in a

cage full of doggies. There were hundreds of

homeless doggies and kitties.

I even got sick and was afraid for my life!

It was a terrifying experience!

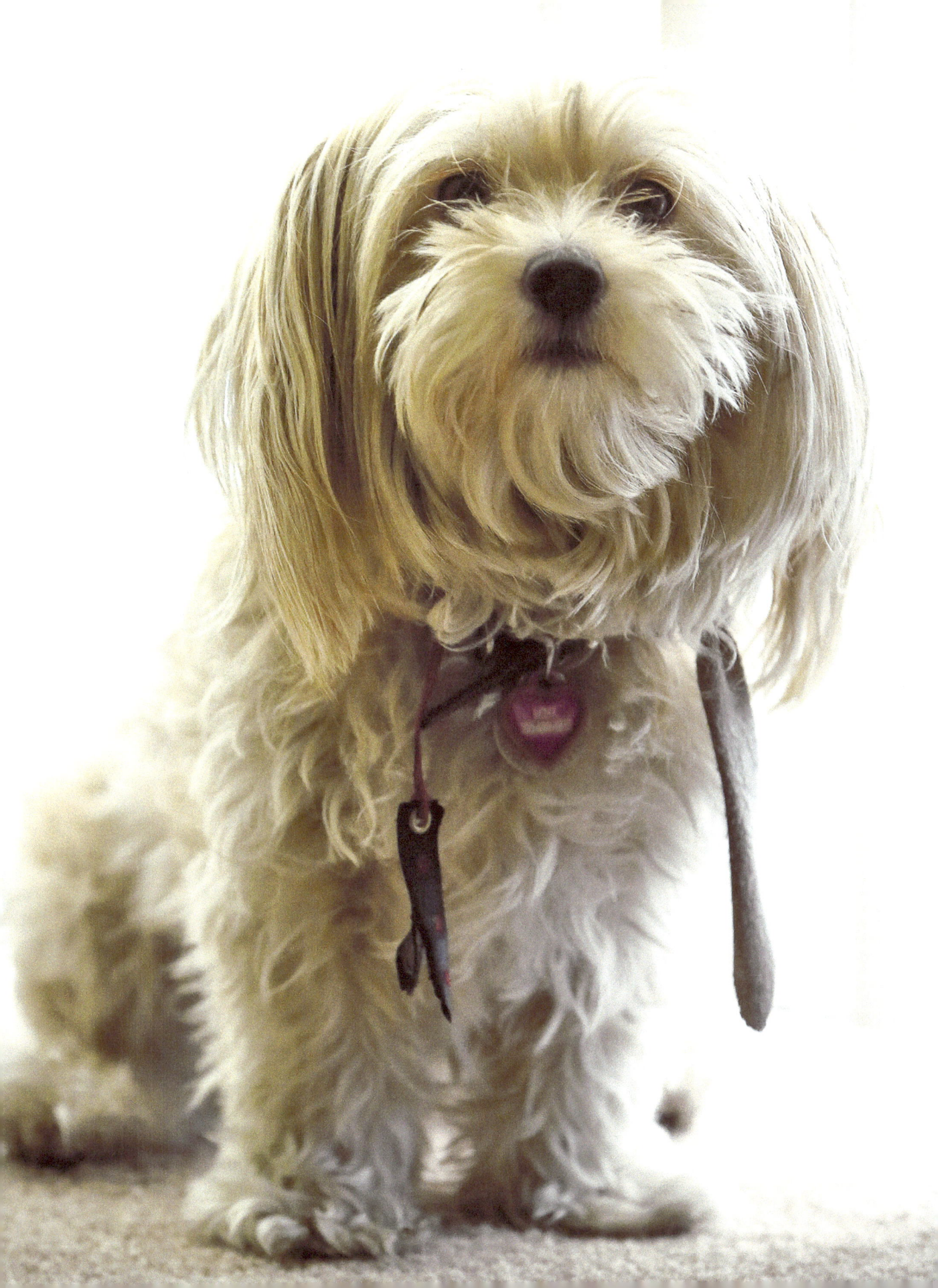

Then one day, a girl came walking by.

She stopped and petted me and comforted me.

Then she took me out of the cage, and

I immediately fell asleep on her lap.

She was sent to be my Guardian Angel,

and I was meant to be hers.

She took me home to her house that day.

I was so happy and relieved!

This was the start of a NEW LIFE!!

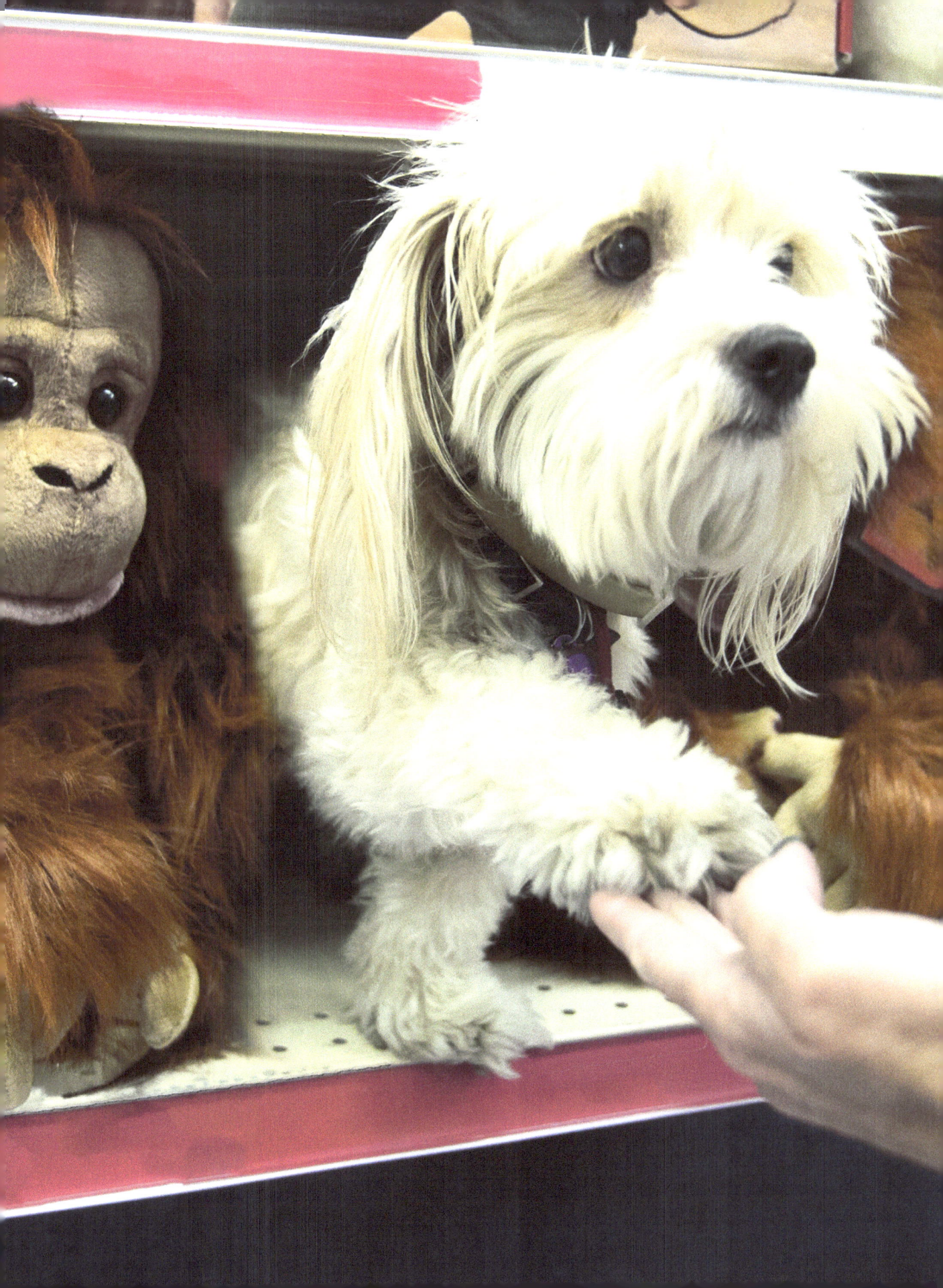

The first thing we did was to go to the store…

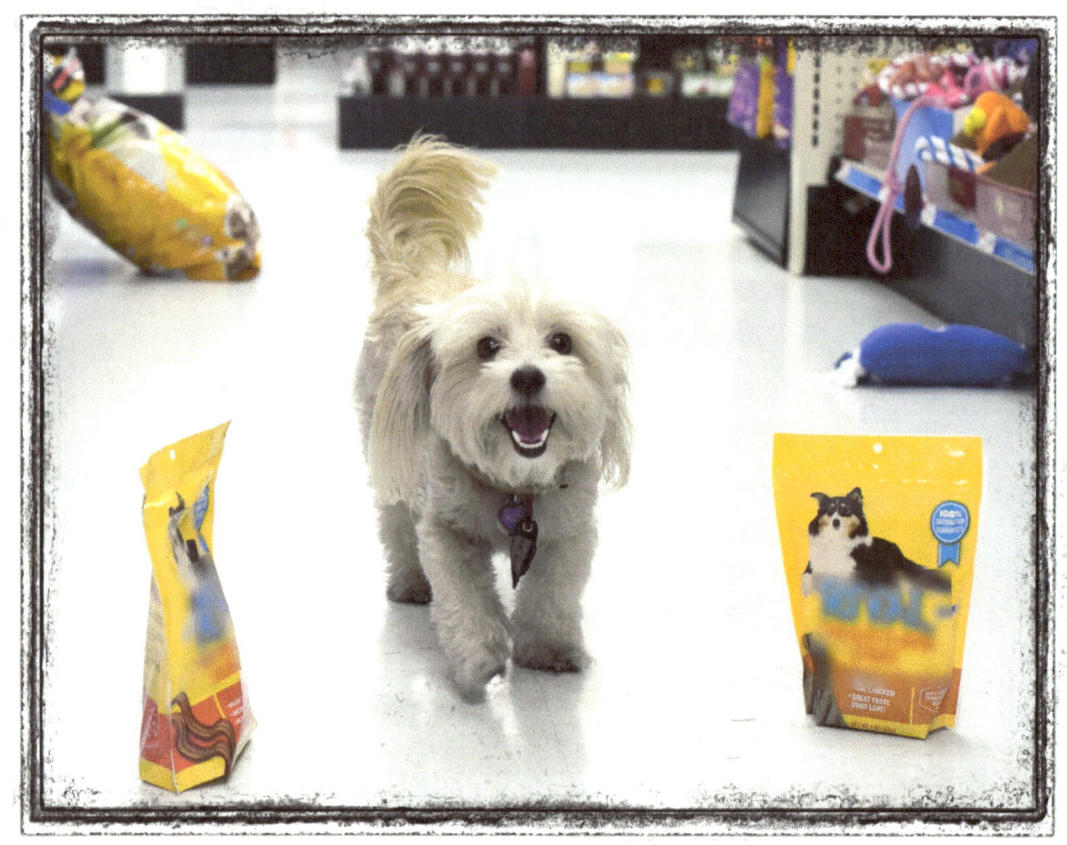

**We picked out food, toys, a collar,
and BONES!!
(My favorite!)**

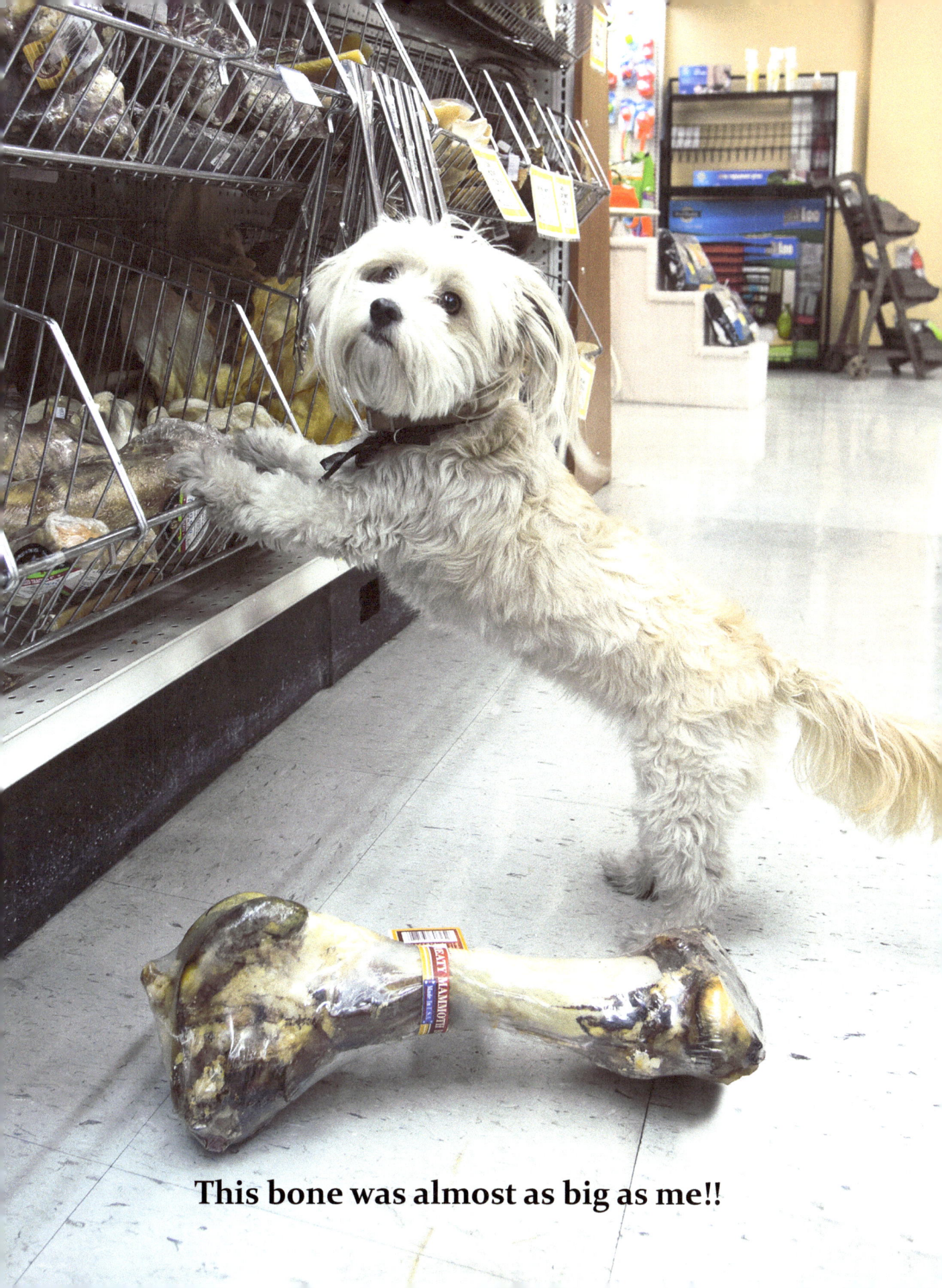

This bone was almost as big as me!!

I was so happy!!
I even did a little show for my mommy!

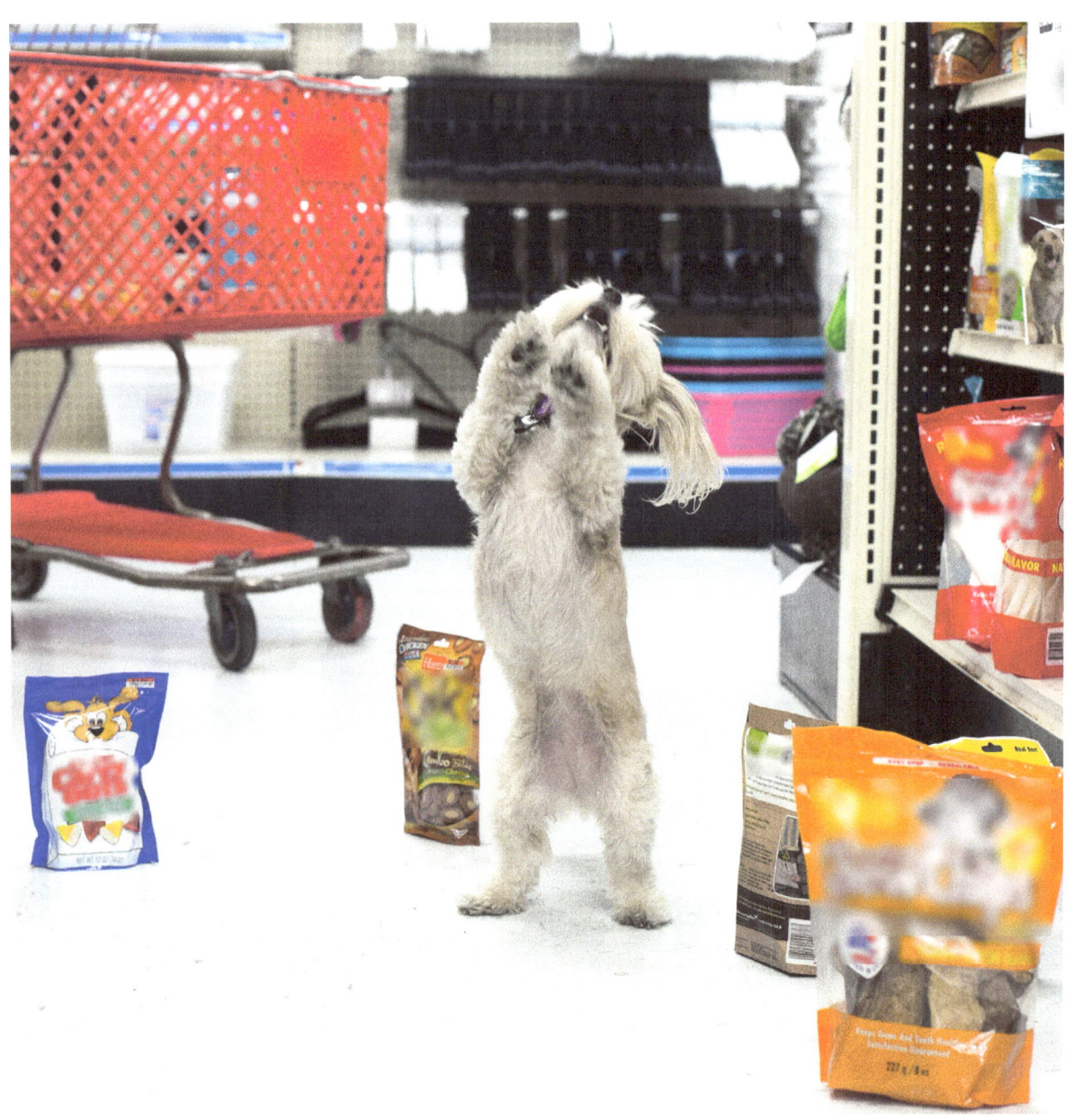

I felt spoiled!

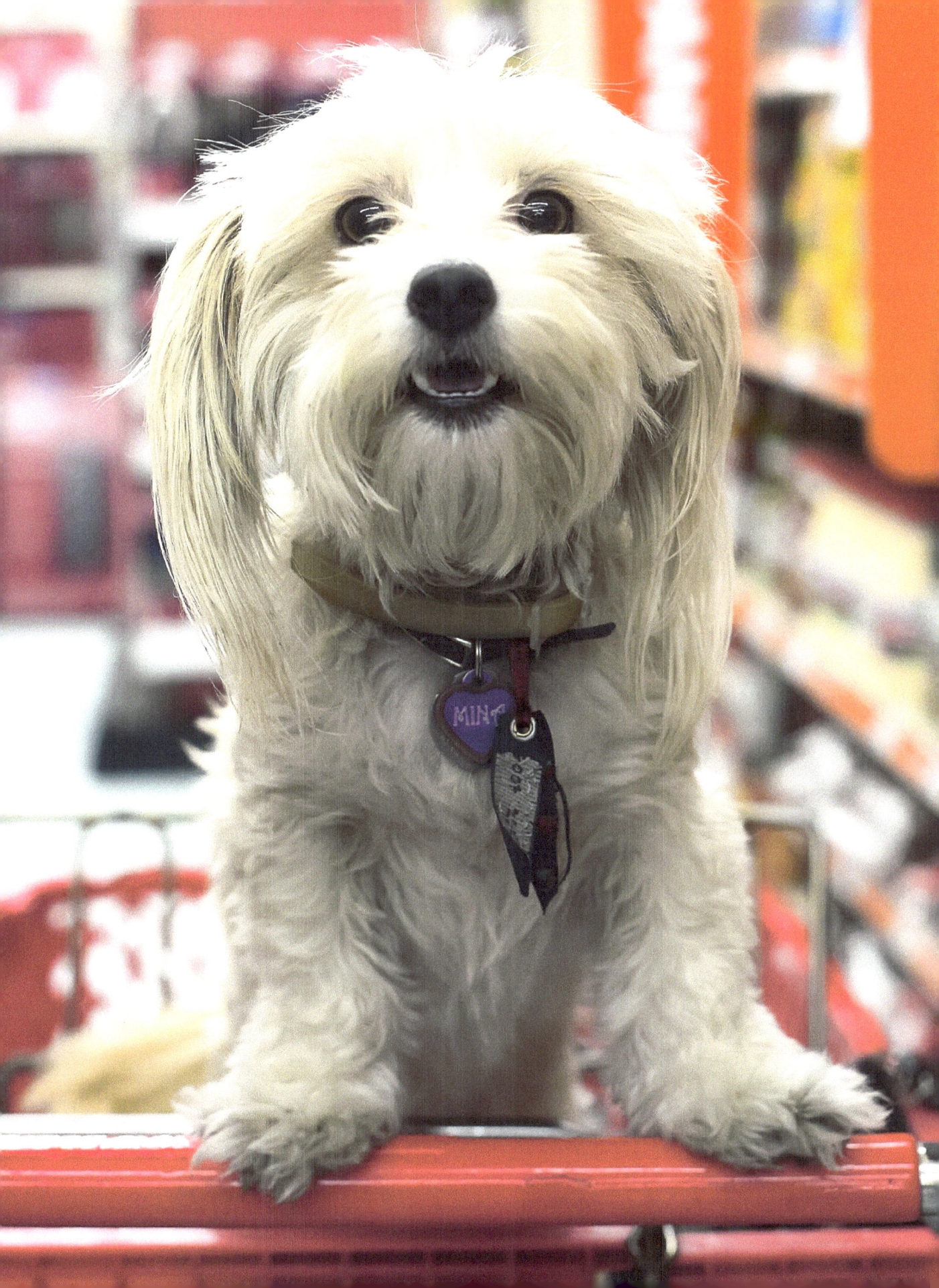

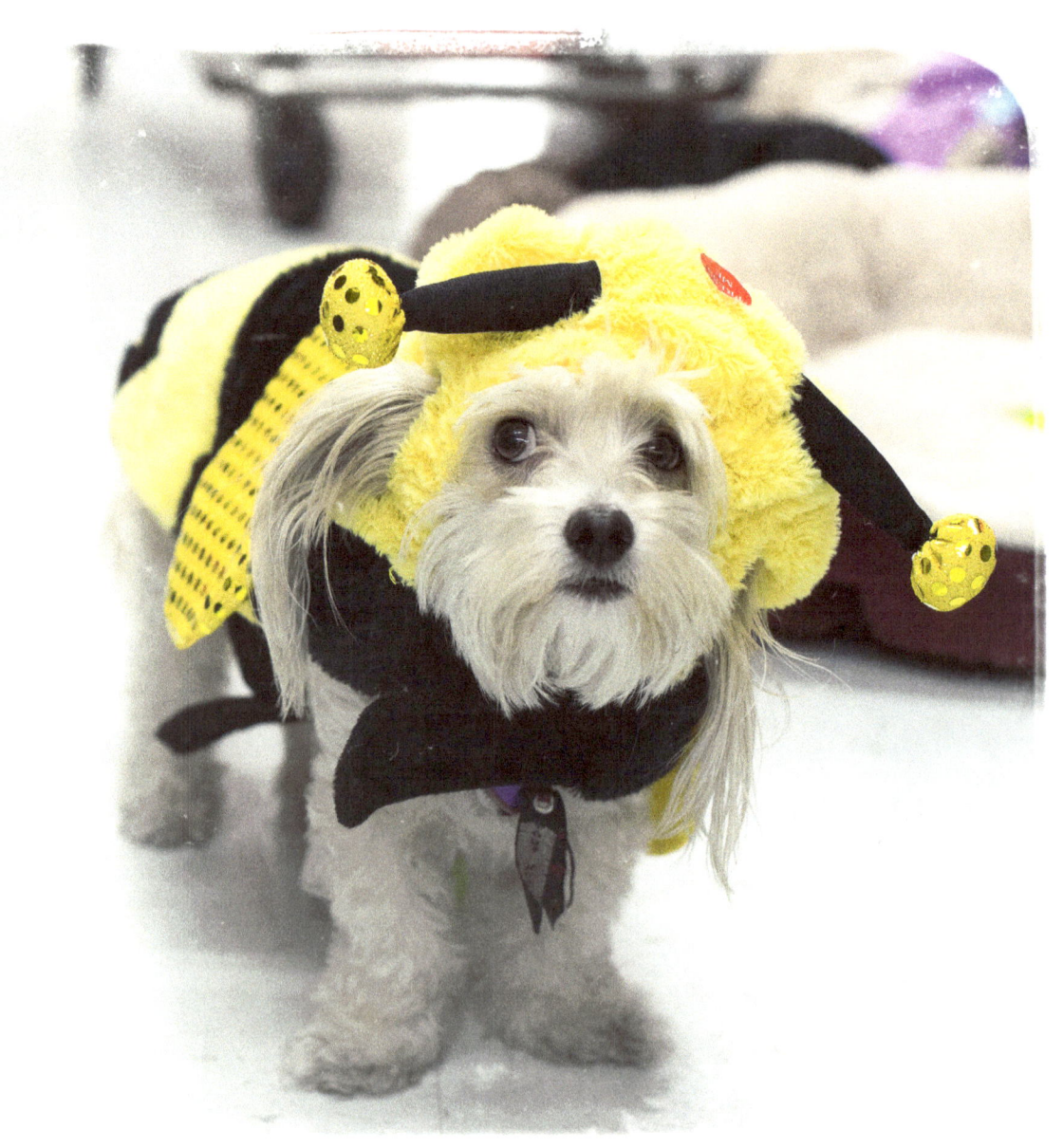

Somehow, I ended up dressed
like a silly bumble-bee.
The humans all thought it was hilarious,
but I was not amused.

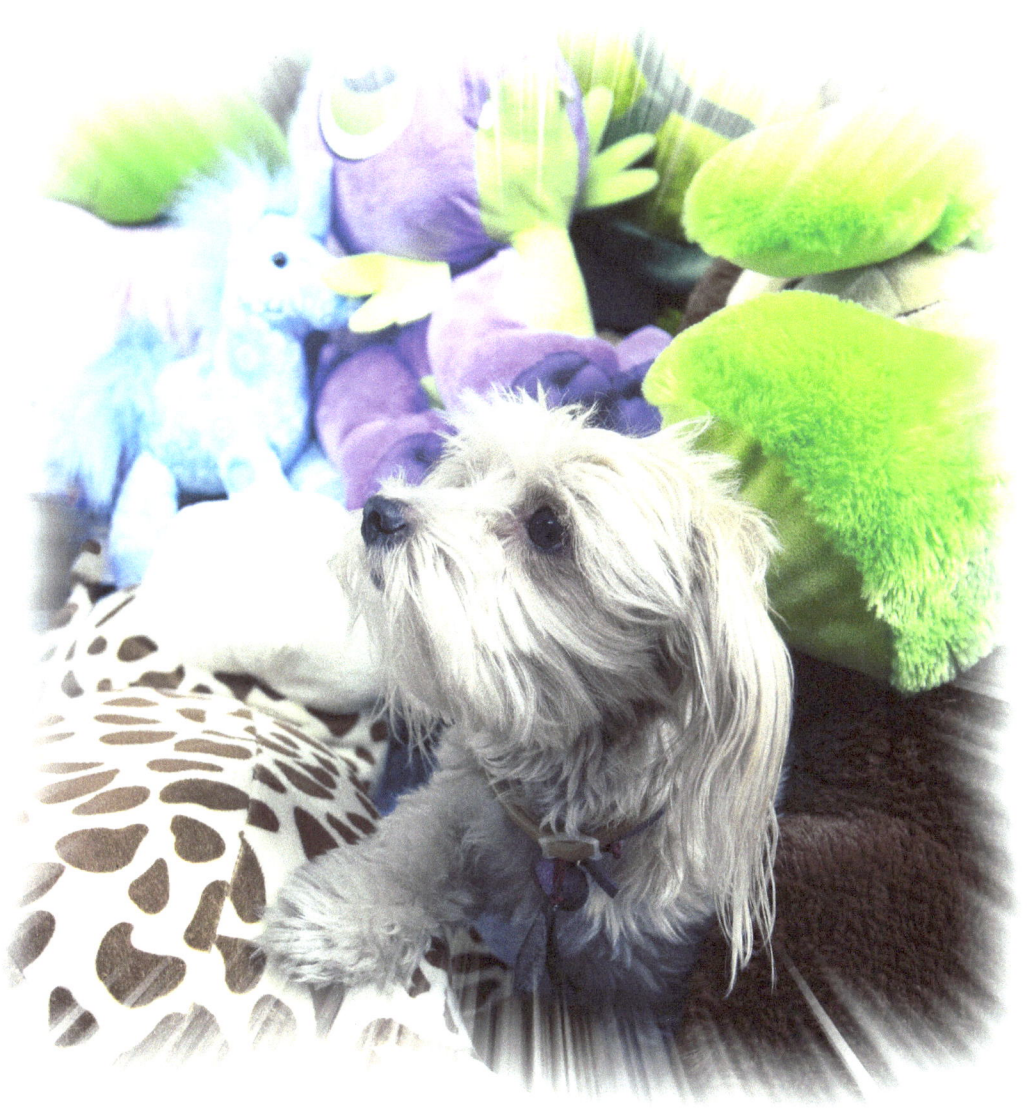

So, I ran around the store and met some
new friends of all shapes and sizes
and hid with them!

Those animals were too quiet for my taste,

so I decided I wanted to go to the beach!

I thought I could make it on this skateboard,

but California is REALLY BIG!

I needed to think of a different way

to get there!

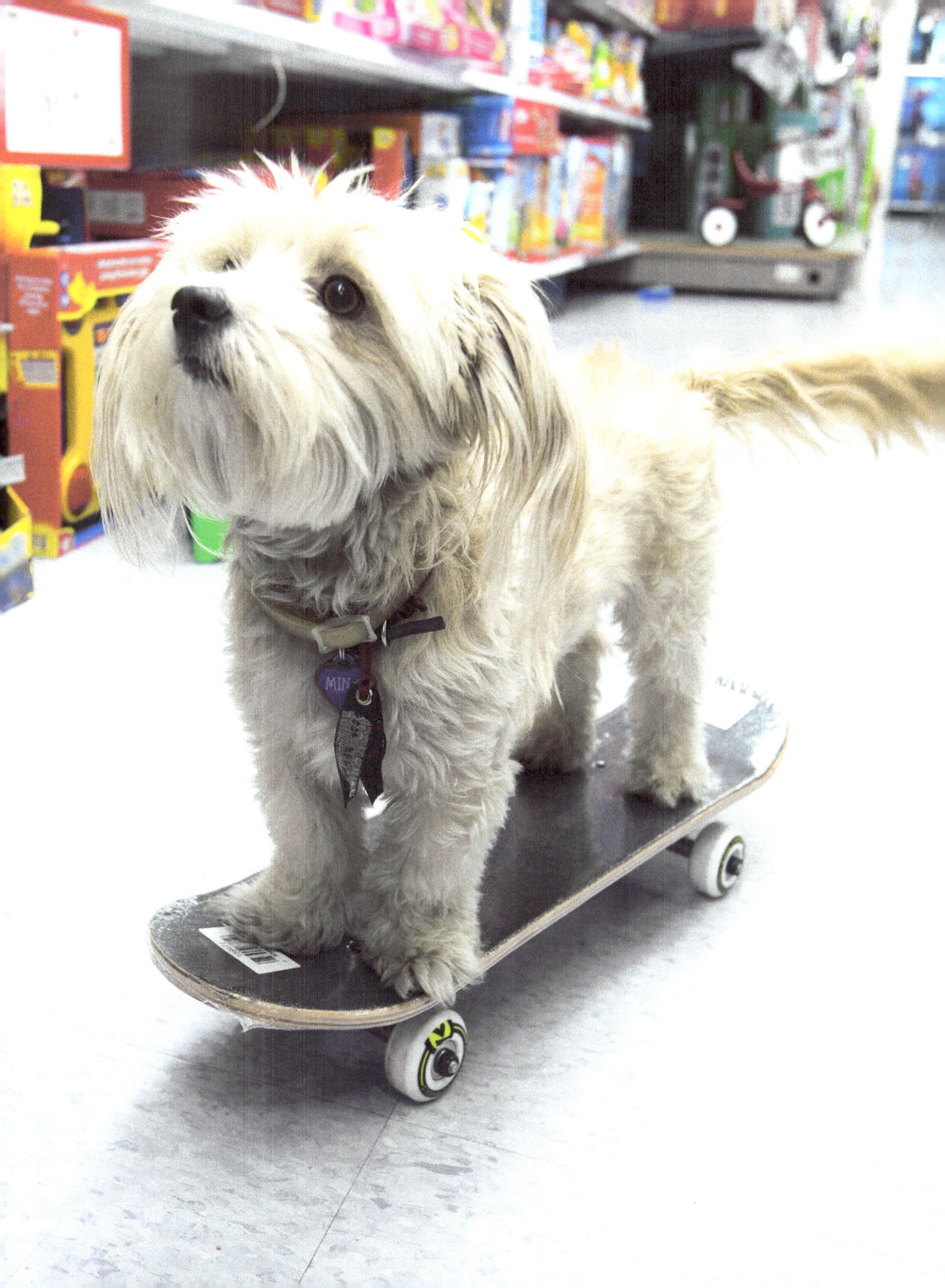

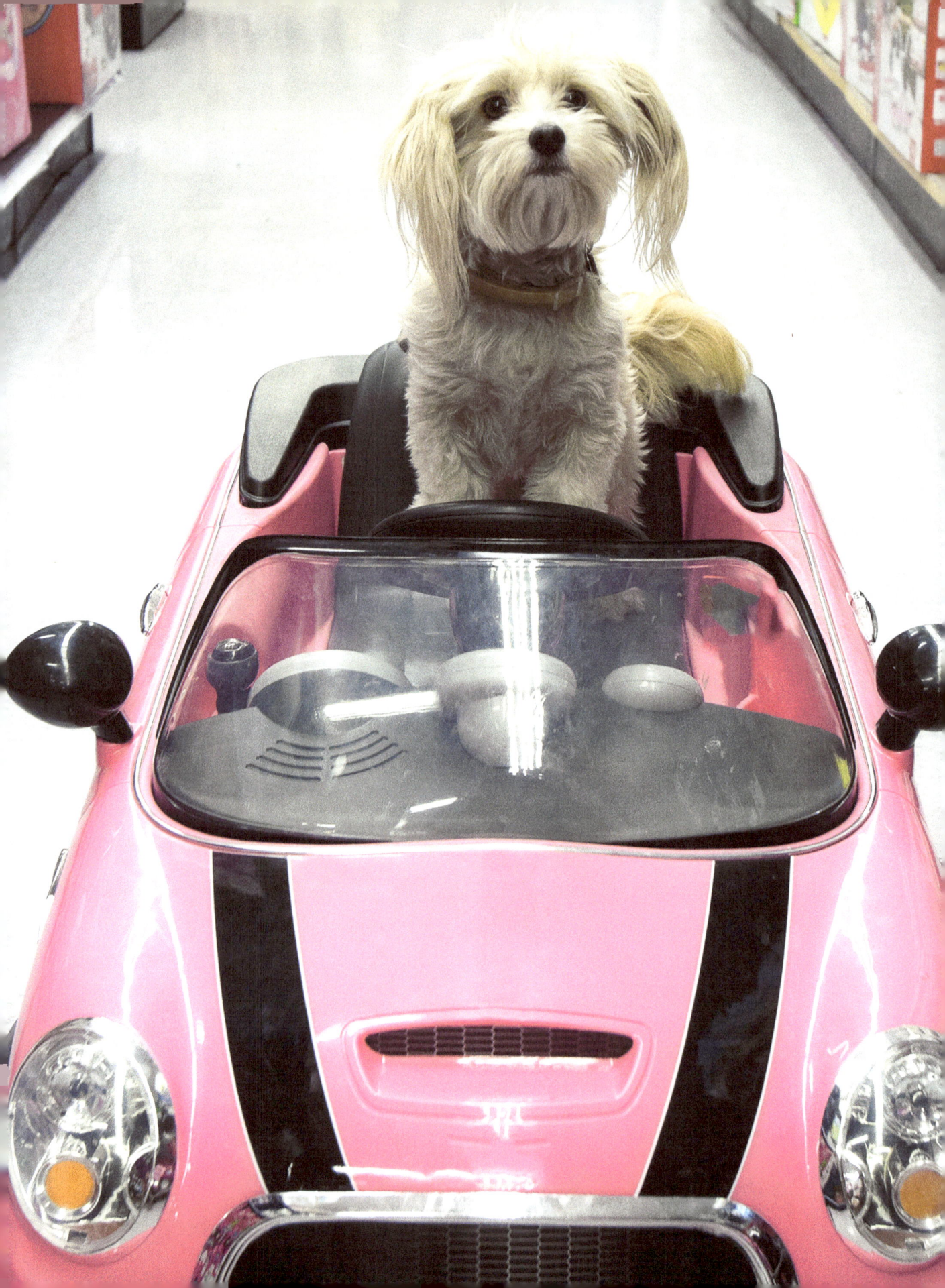

I decided to get a little pink car!

After a quick test-drive around the aisles,

I thought this one was perfect for me!

I knew it would be a pretty smooth drive with

this nice convertible!

I loved it!

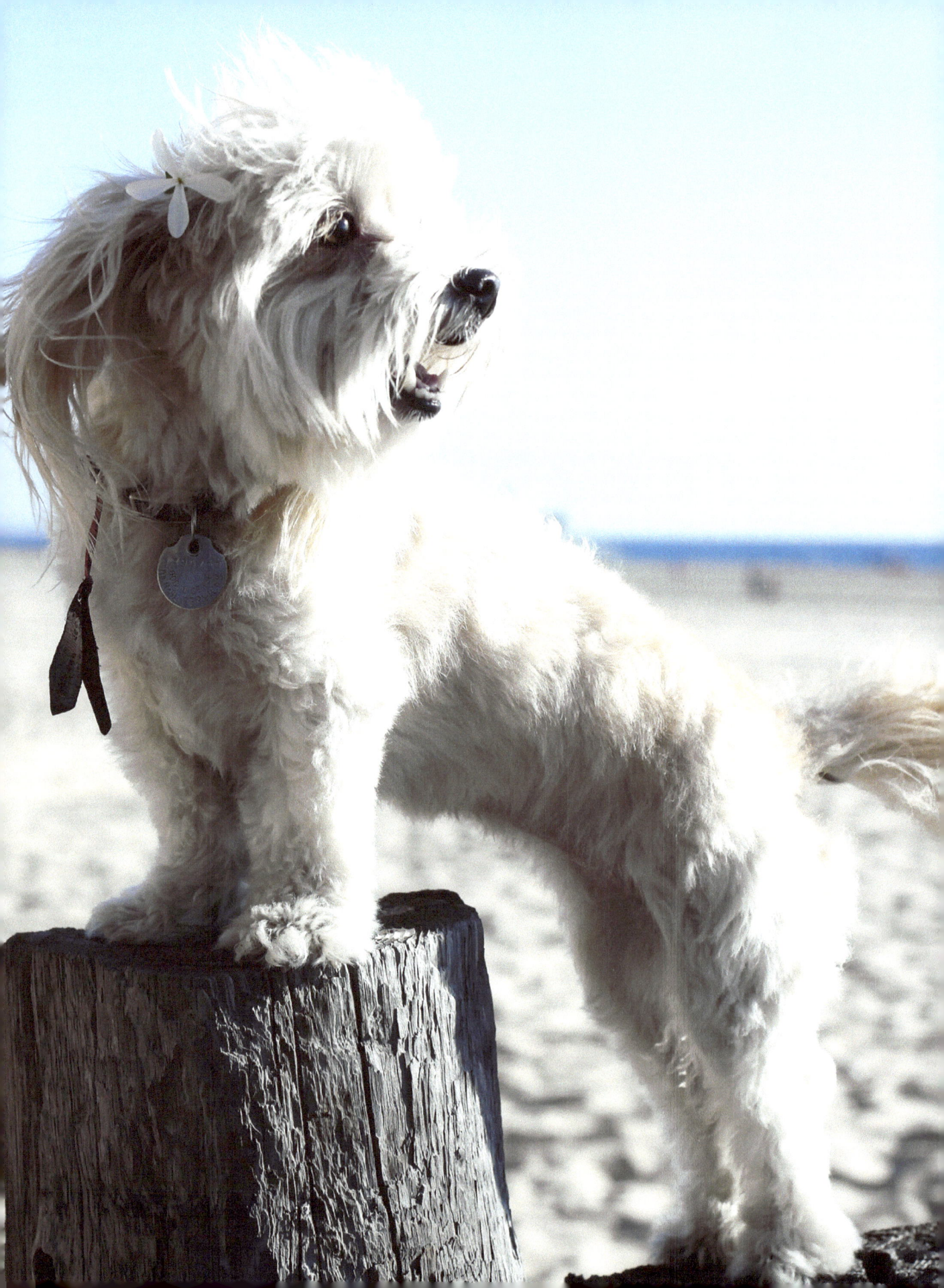

I arrived quickly in my race car

and admired the beach

near the marina of Los Angeles!

This beach was pretty nice!

Yet, I wanted to see what was

further up the coast.

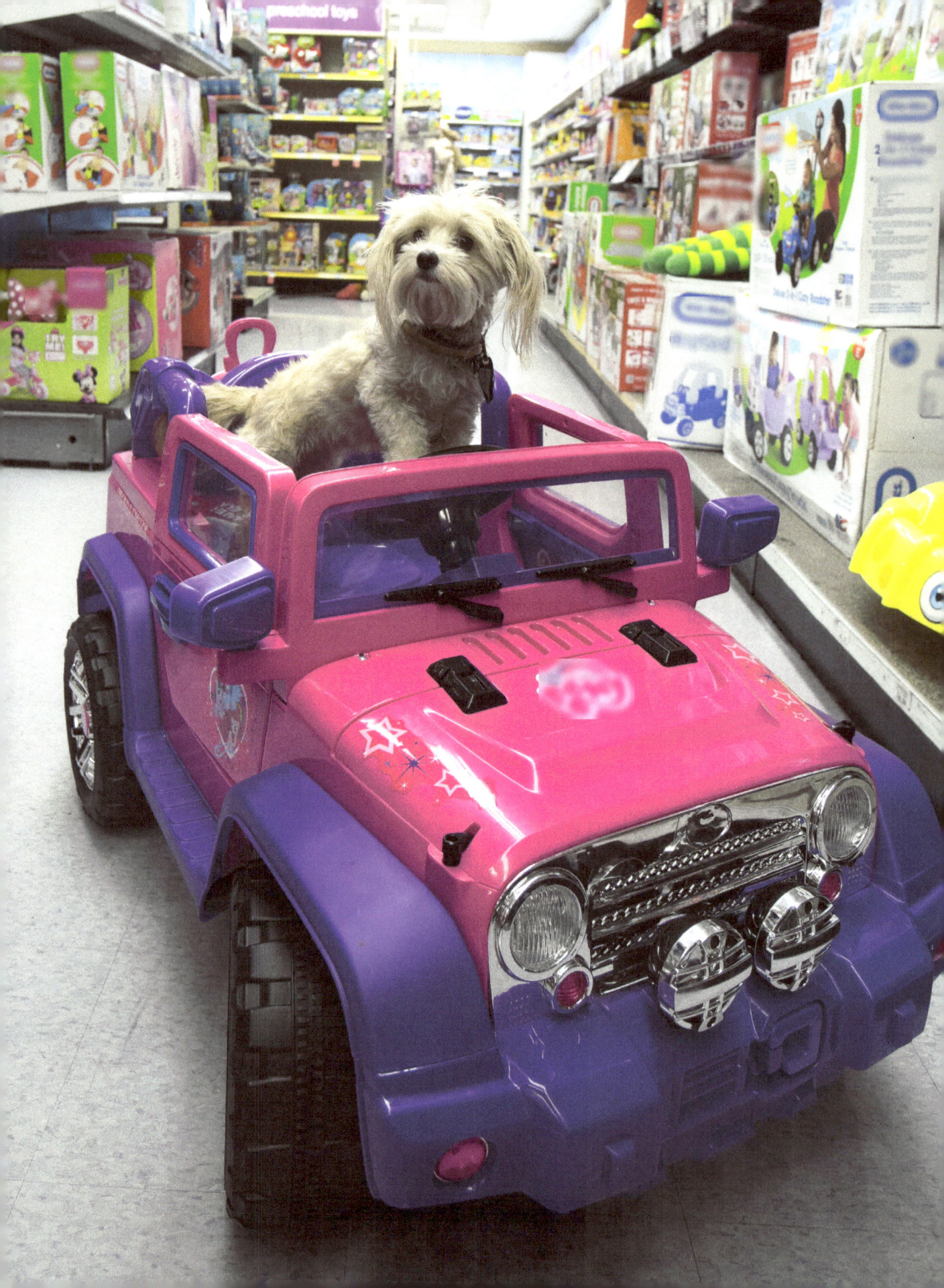

I heard the most beautiful beaches are in

Malibu!

I thought the roads might get rough

up the coast, we may need a truck to get

all the way up there!

I went back to the toy store/car dealership

and found something a little bigger

and stronger for my next adventure!

I thought this truck would do the job!!

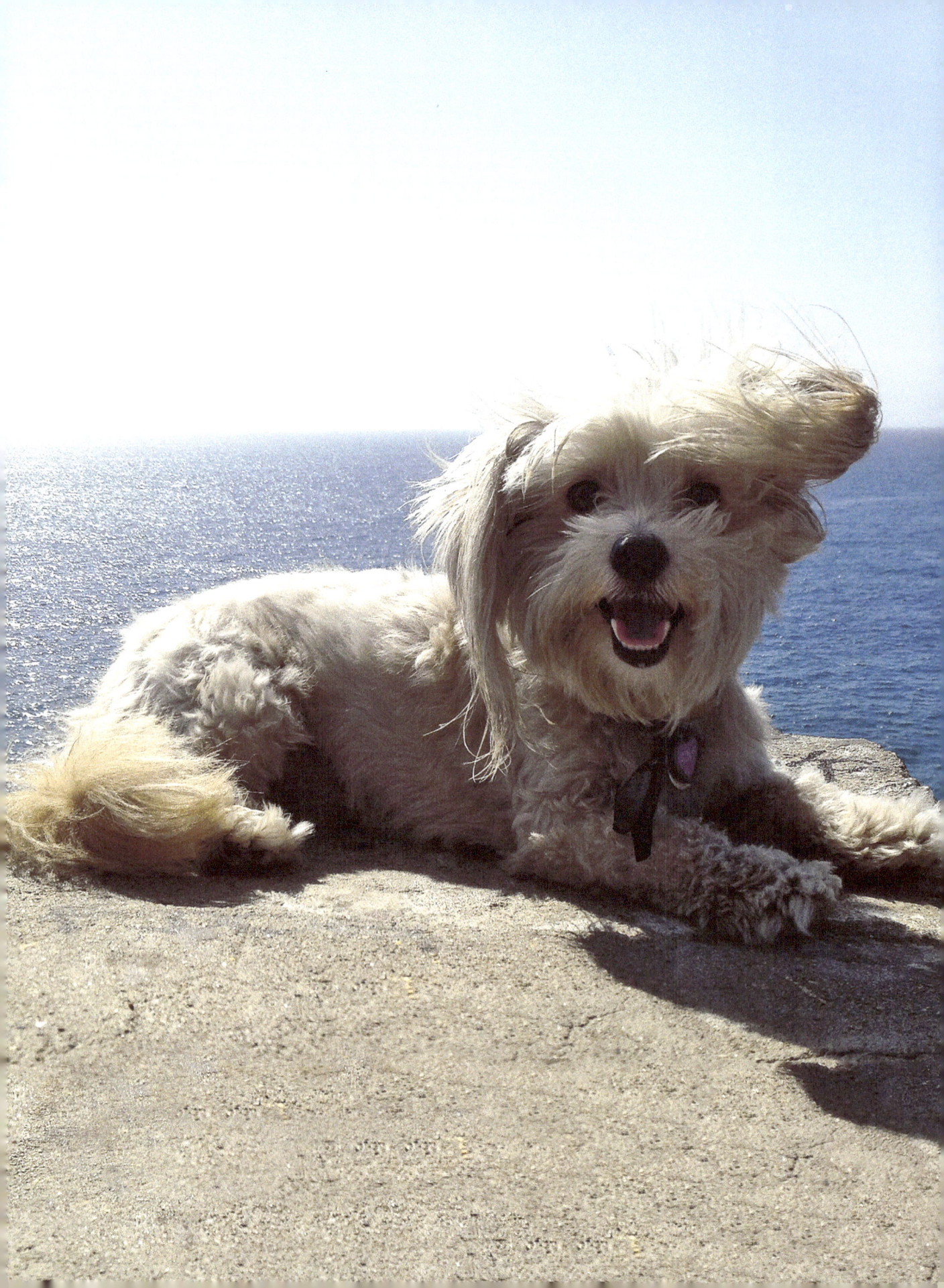

I finally made it to Point Dume in Malibu!!

I was up on a high cliff looking

down at the beautiful ocean!

I could even see dolphins and seals from there!

Every year, at certain times,

the whales swim by as they migrate

to and from Mexico.

This is my favorite beach!

I was so happy!!

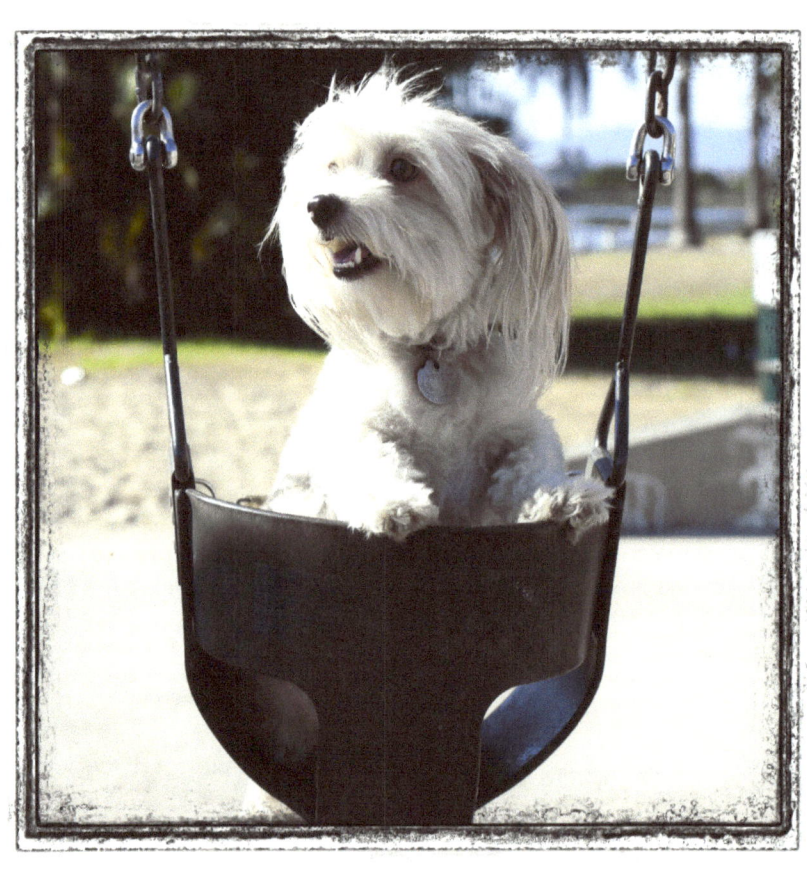

On the way home, we stopped at the playground!
I loved swinging high and sliding down
the sliding board!

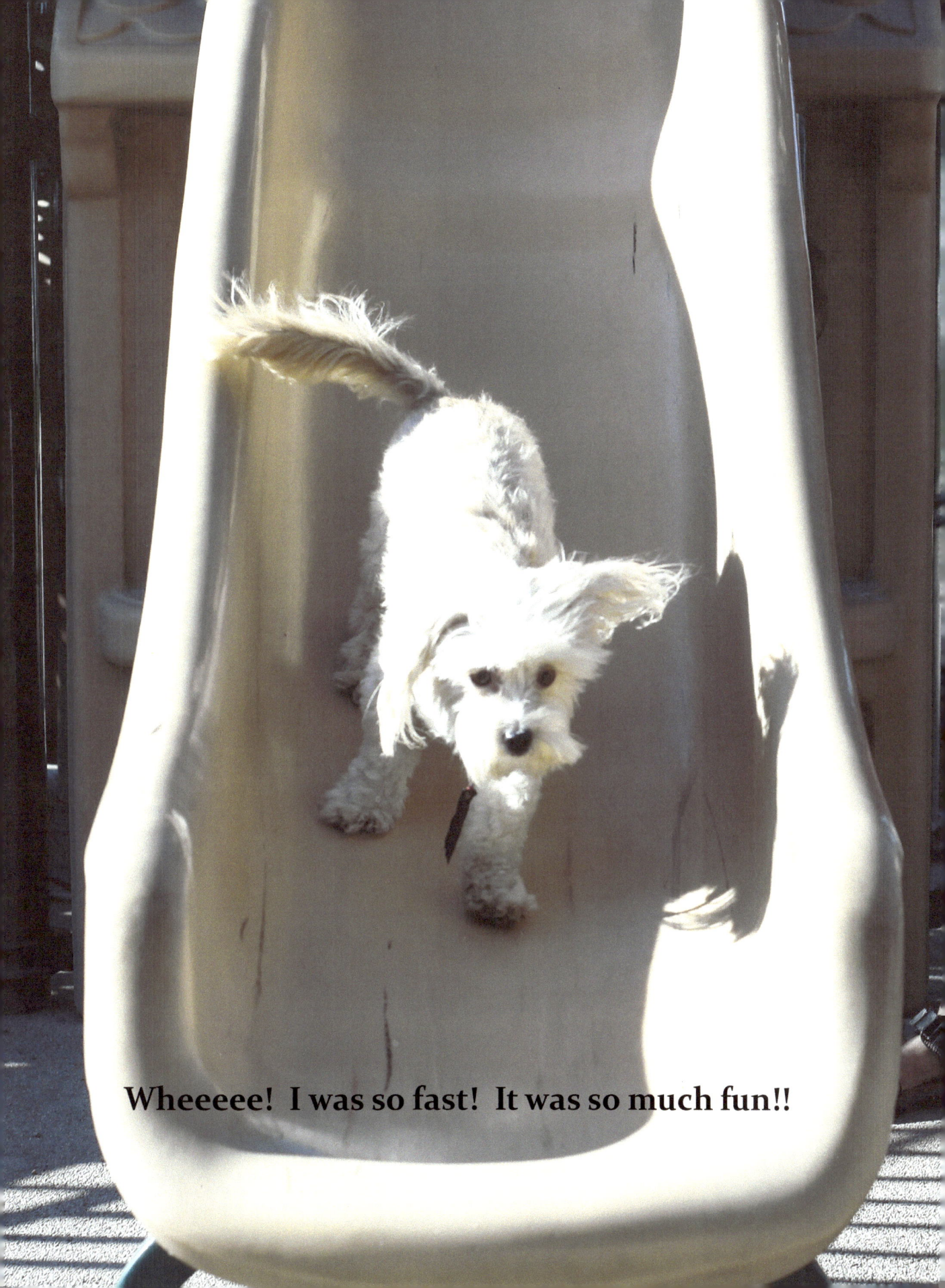

Wheeeee! I was so fast! It was so much fun!!

Then I got to do one of my favorite things

in the whole, wide world...

I CHASED BIRDS!!!!

I felt like I could fly with them!

I was so fast!

I almost caught them all!!

Also, I had a little admirer!

He was impressed at how fast I could run!

Don't tell anyone,

but I love little black doggies!

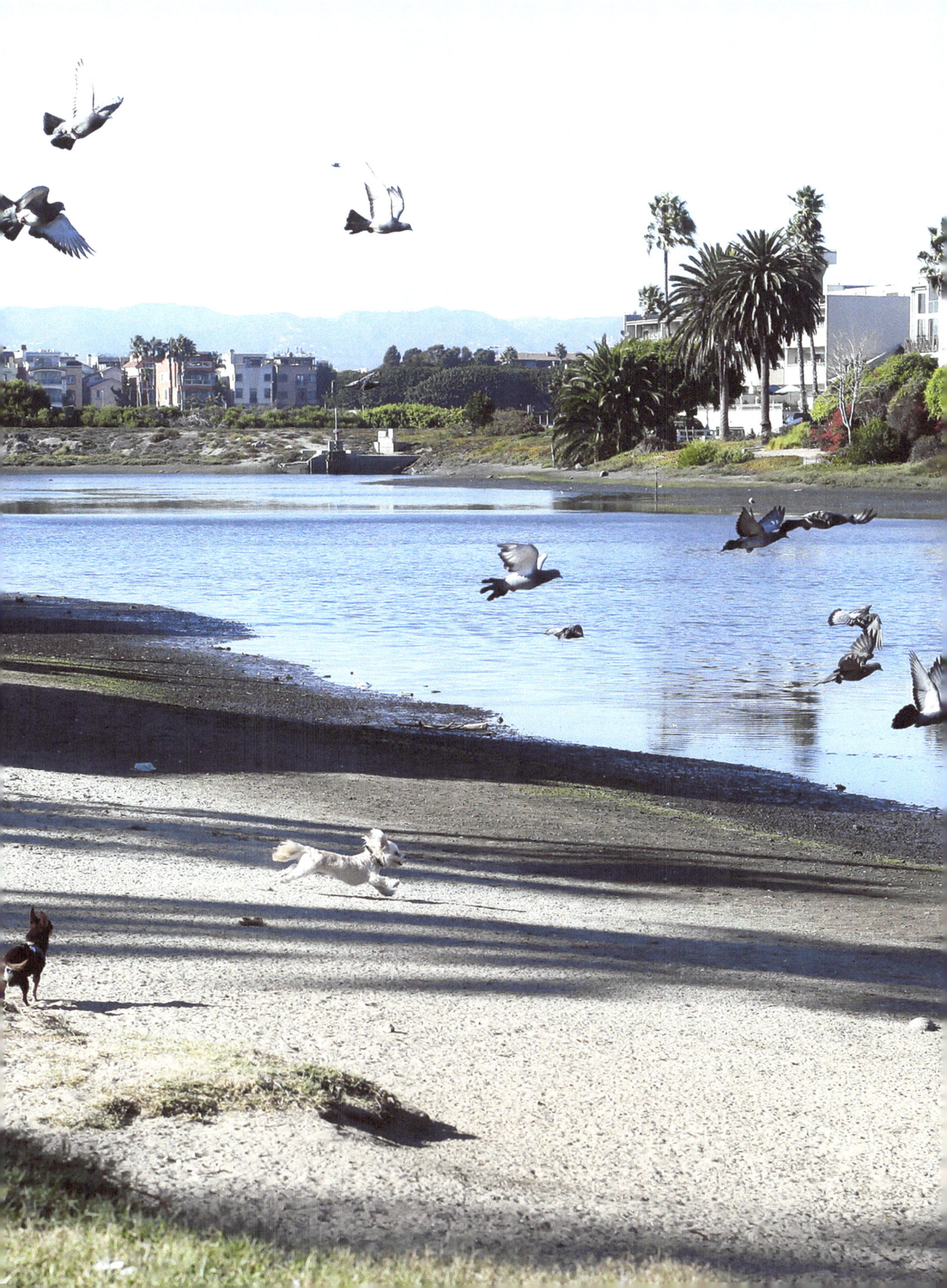

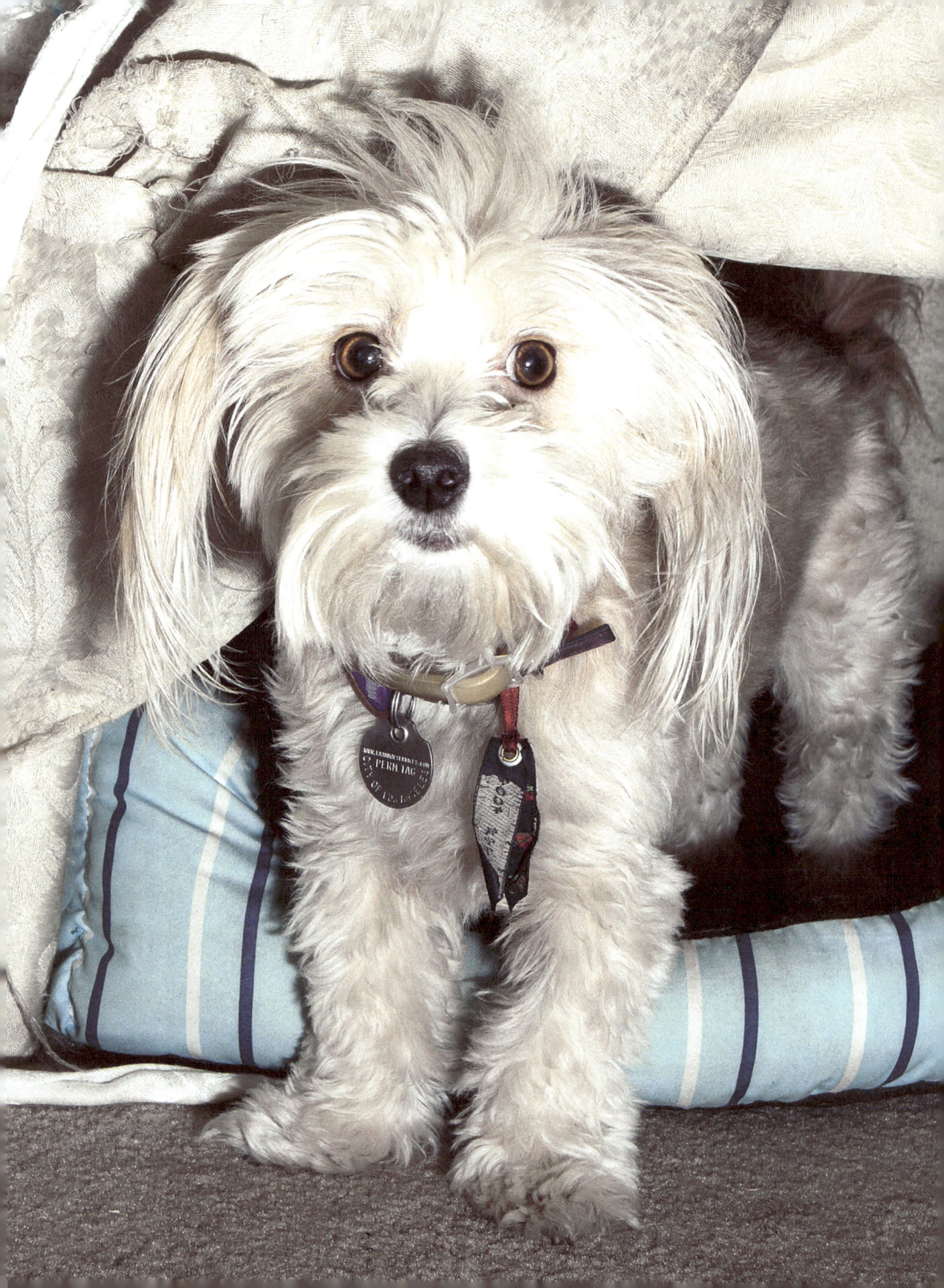

Chasing birds made me very tired!

When we got back home, I went into

my canopy bed to take a cat-nap.

It is very comfy in there!

It is my own little fort!

Nobody even knows I'm there!

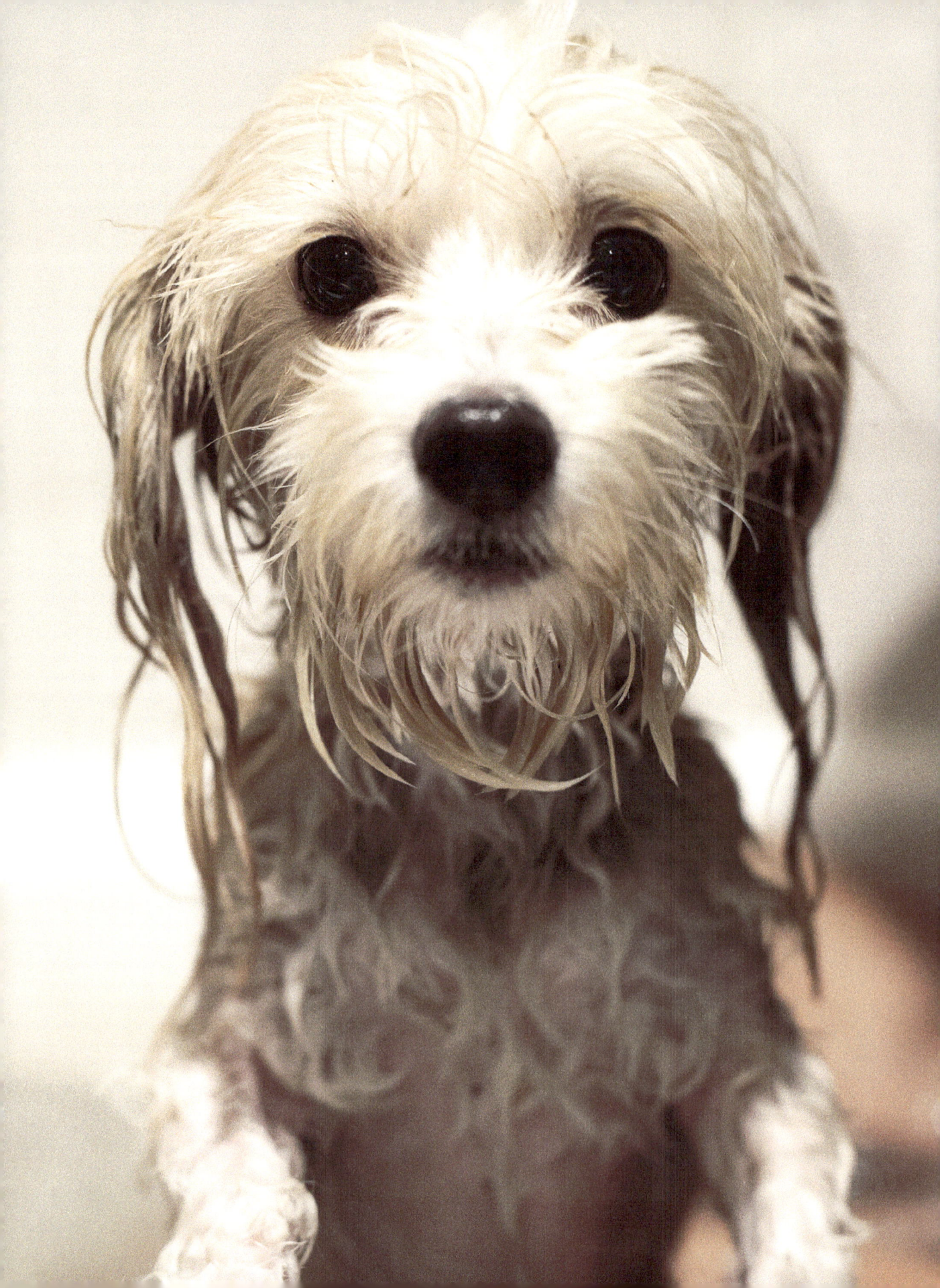

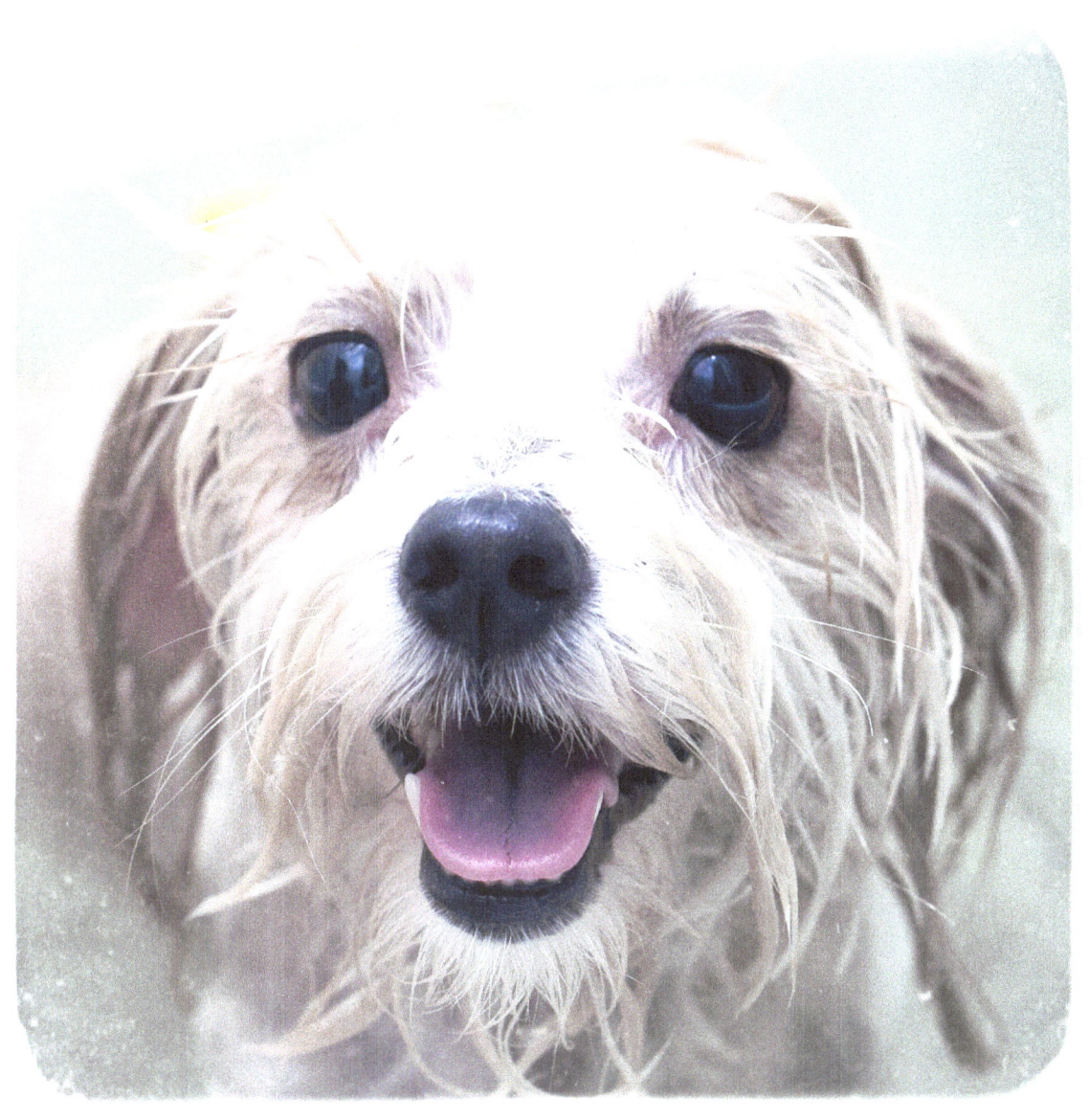

When I woke up,
my mommy gave me a bath.

I do not like taking baths but they make me so clean,
and I smell nice too!

Then I got ready for the evening.

I am really quite a remarkable being!

Sometimes, when I look in the mirror,

I am confused as to whether I am a dog

or a beautiful princess!

I am so very lucky!

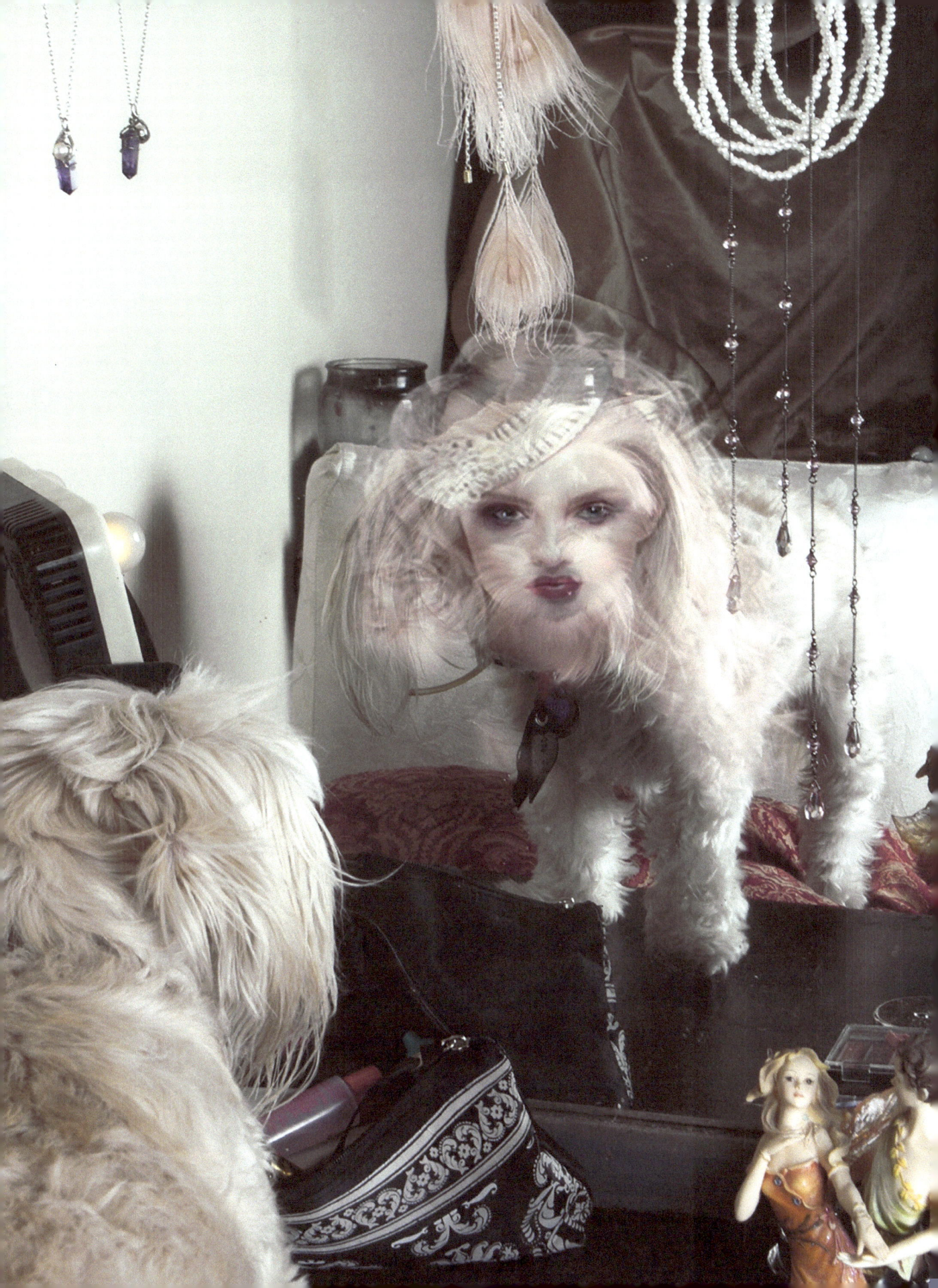

I am also very smart!

I love to read books bigger than me!!

This one will take me a long time!

I am only on page four...

The letters are so small that I have to borrow

Mommy's glasses to read them!

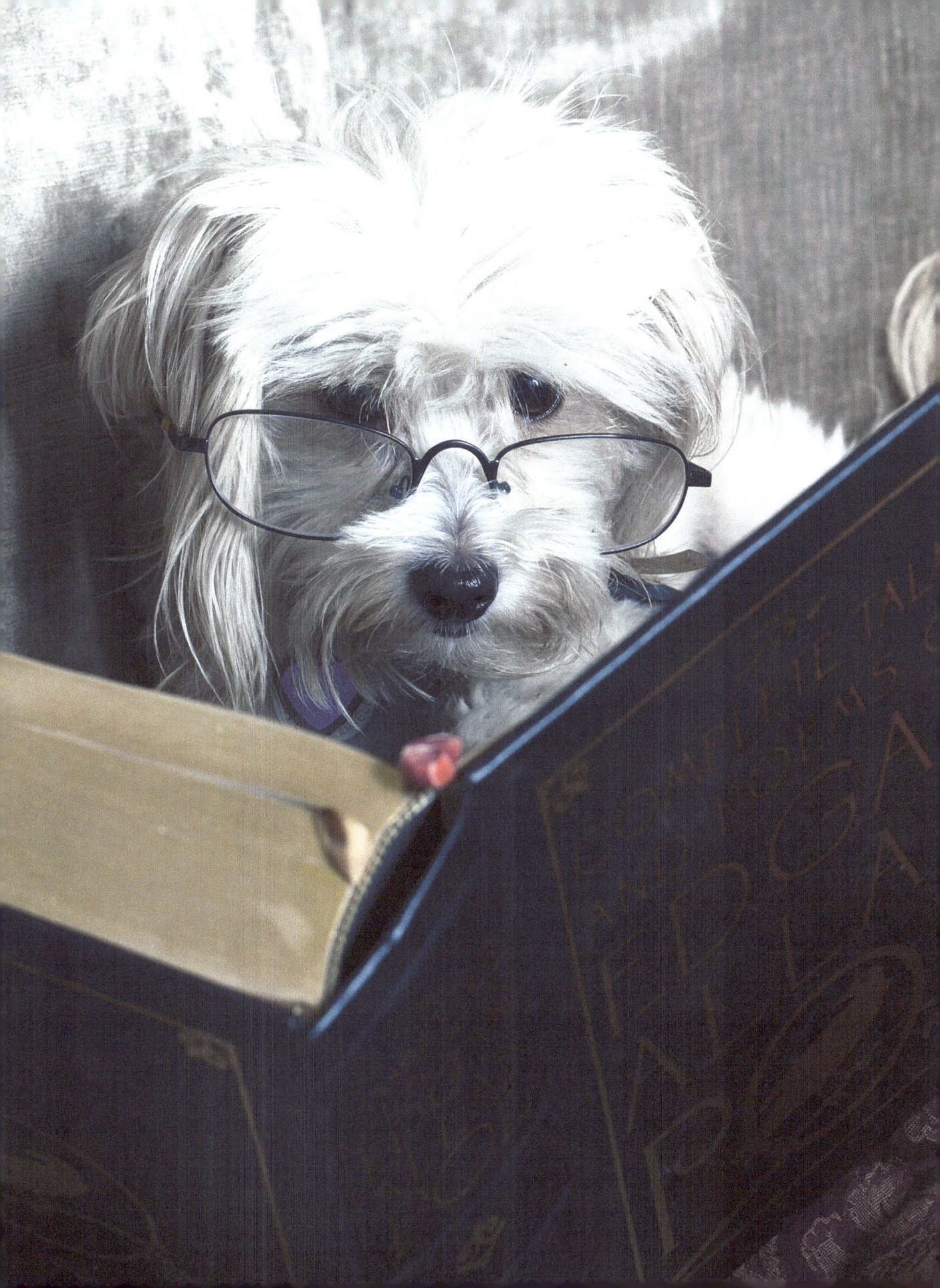

I also love playing chess with my

friend and roomate, Bozo,

the Funny Monkey!

He's been living with us for as

long as I can remember!

He doesn't talk very much but

he makes me laugh a lot,

and we love to play games together!!

He is good at clapping his cymbals

together, but I always win the

chess game!

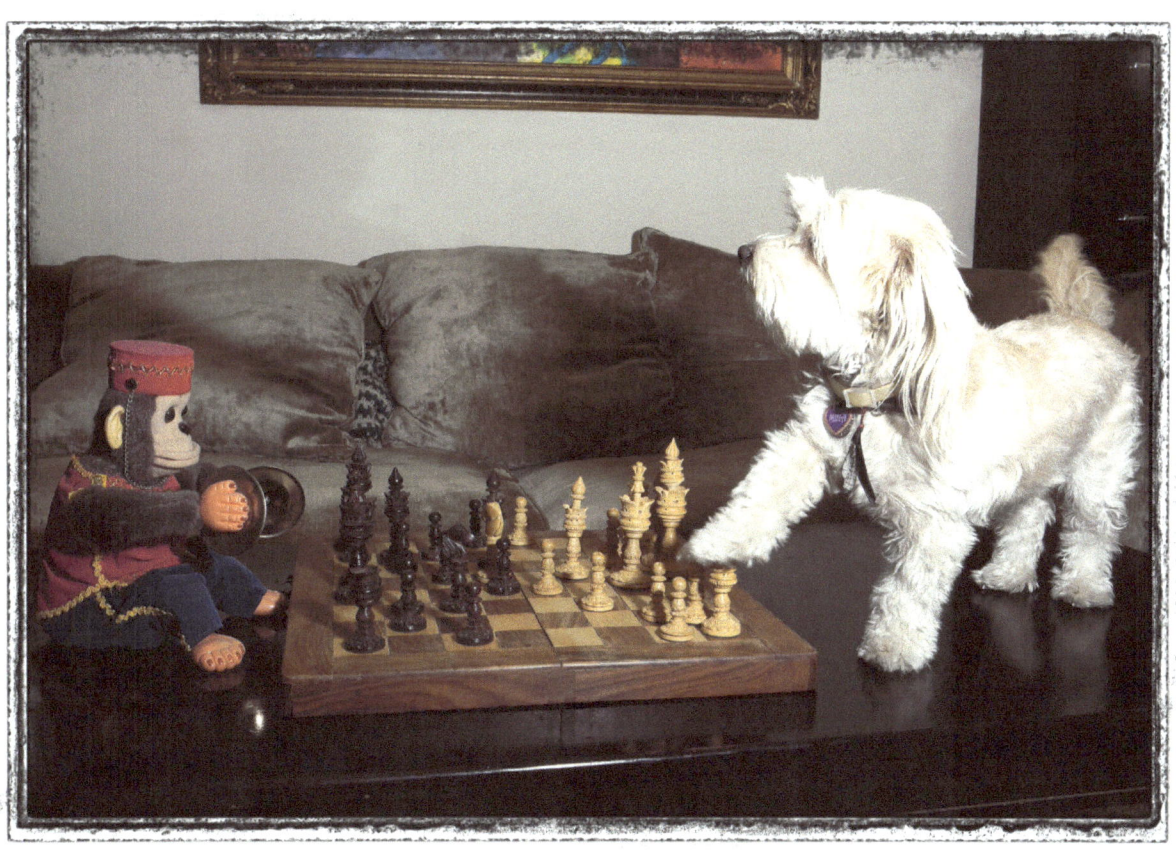

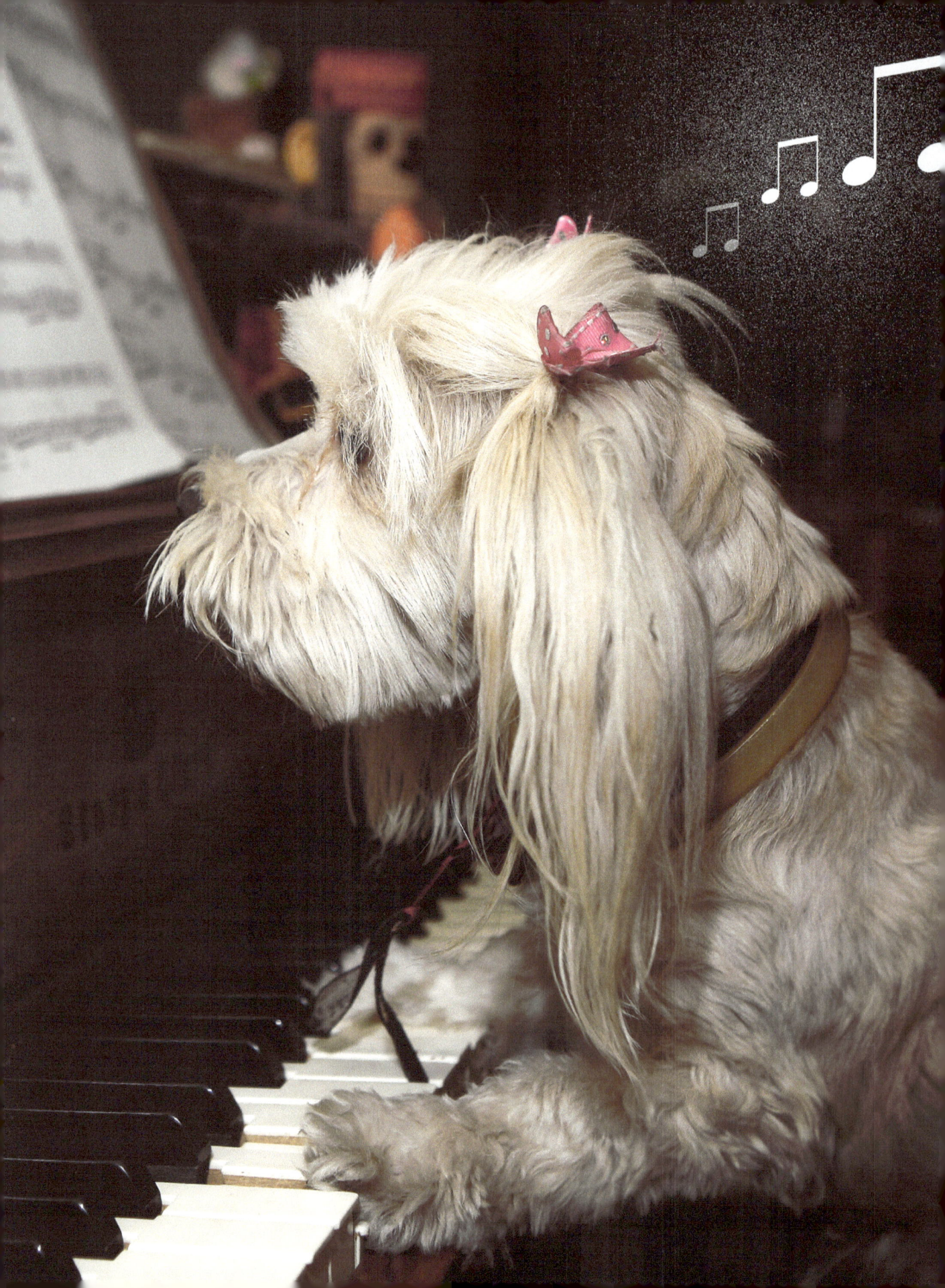

After the chess game, I played Johann Pachelbel's "Canon in D." I think I did pretty well for a little creature like myself, but I admit that I missed a few notes because I do not have thumbs.

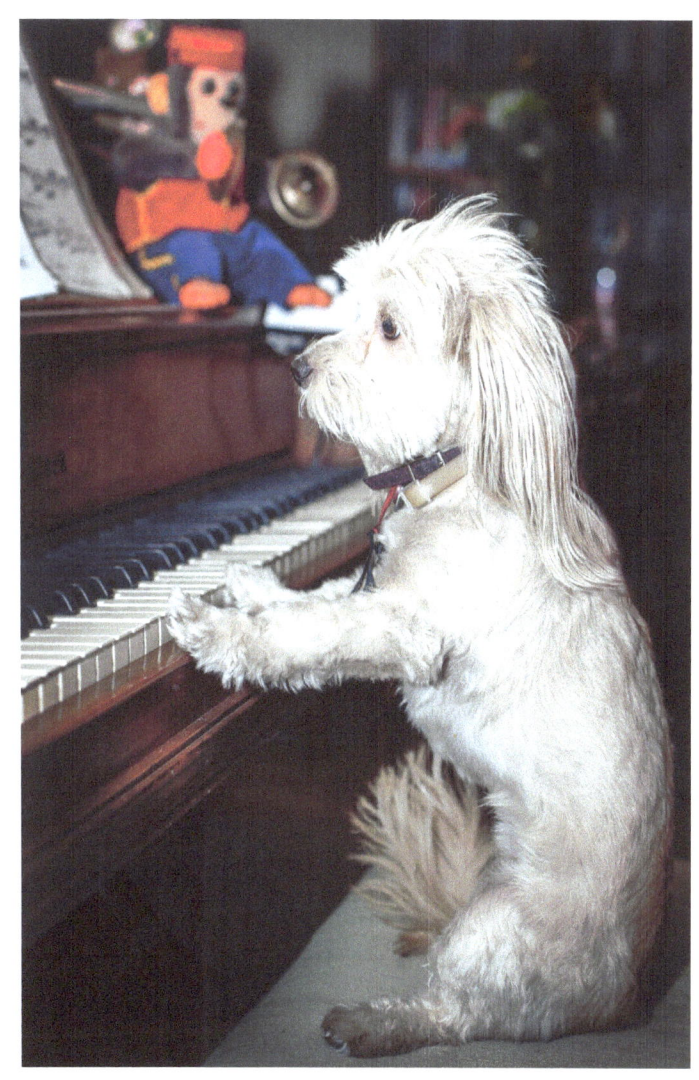

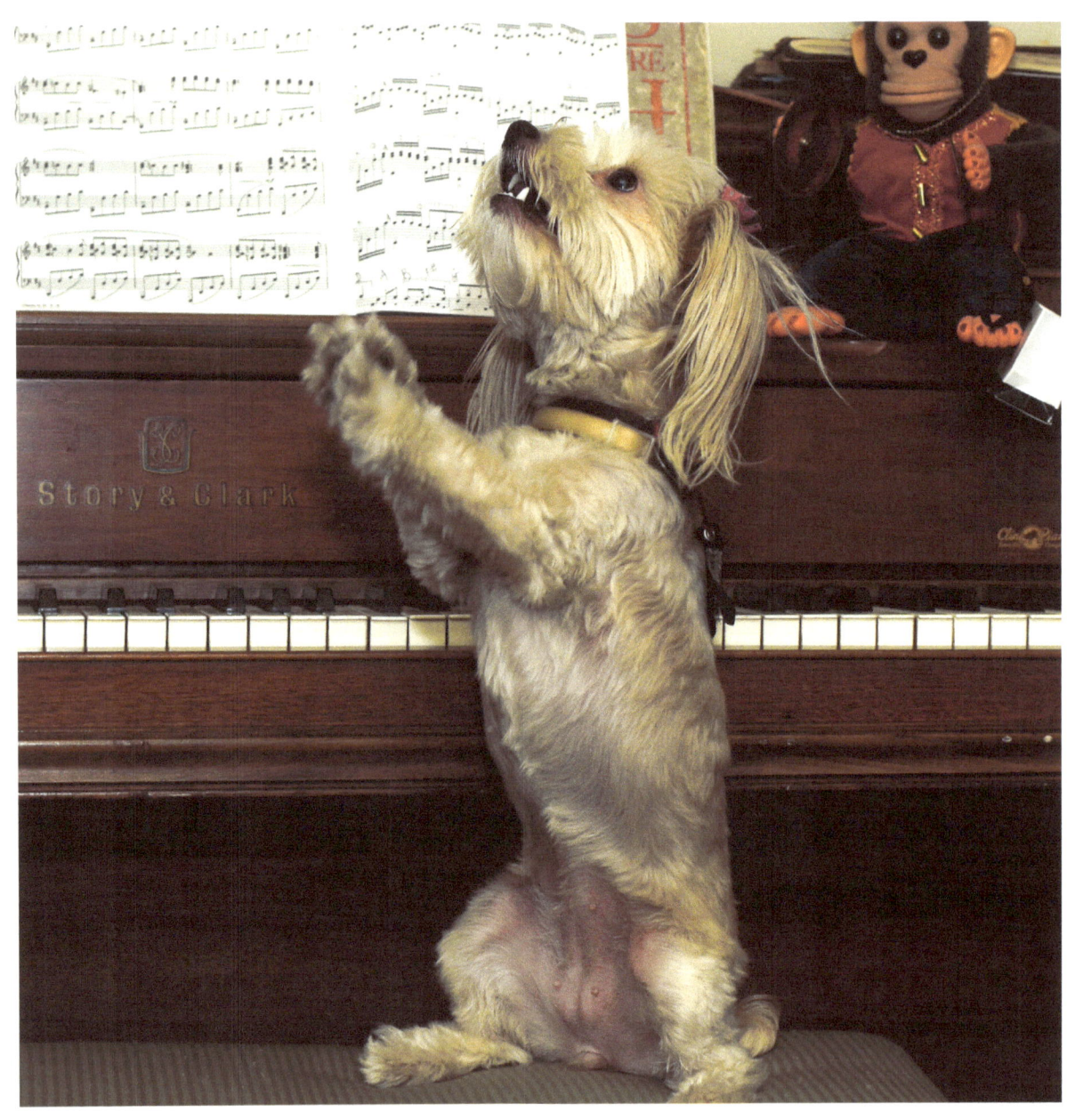

Even Bozo clapped for me!
(Everybody, clap for Mina!!!!)

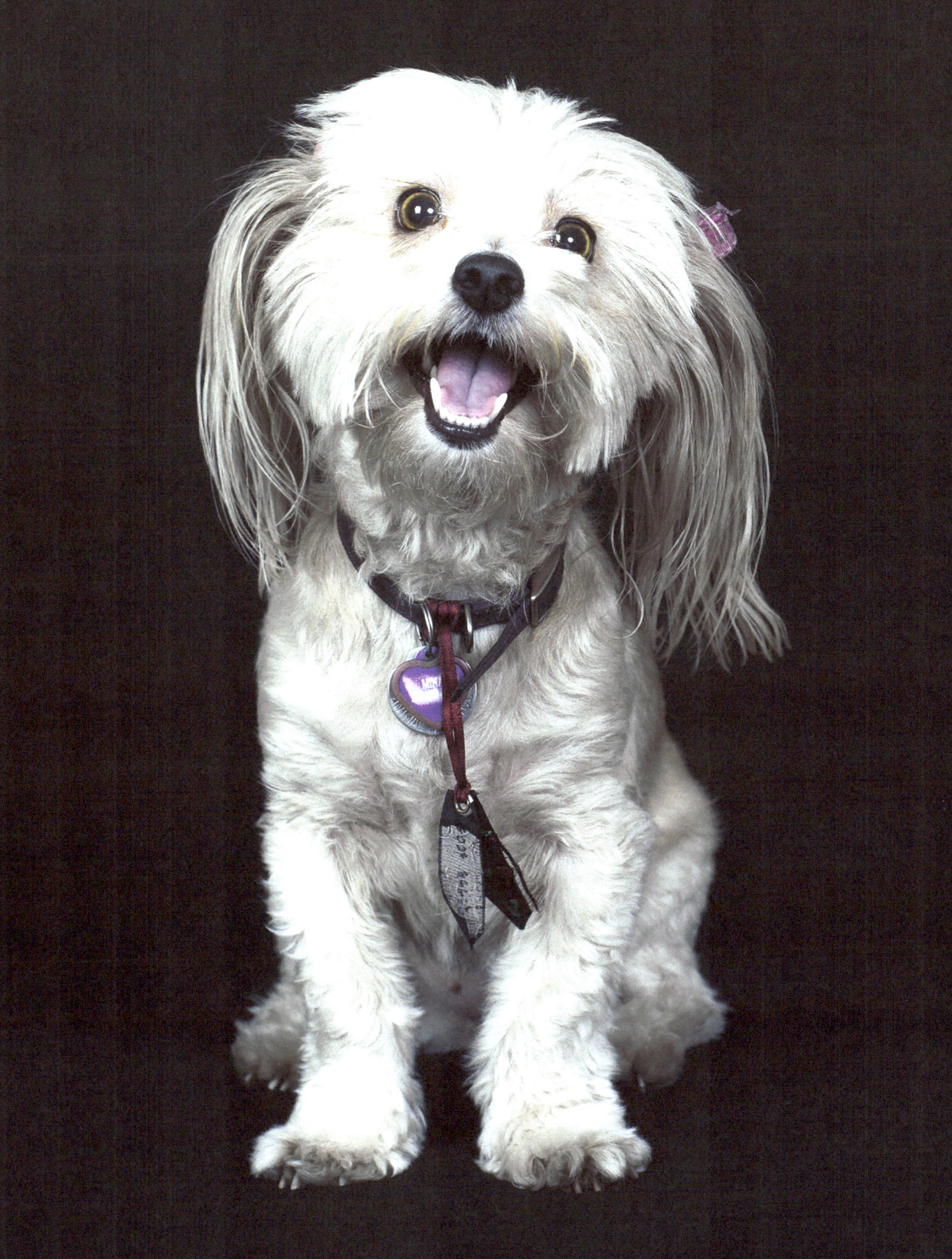

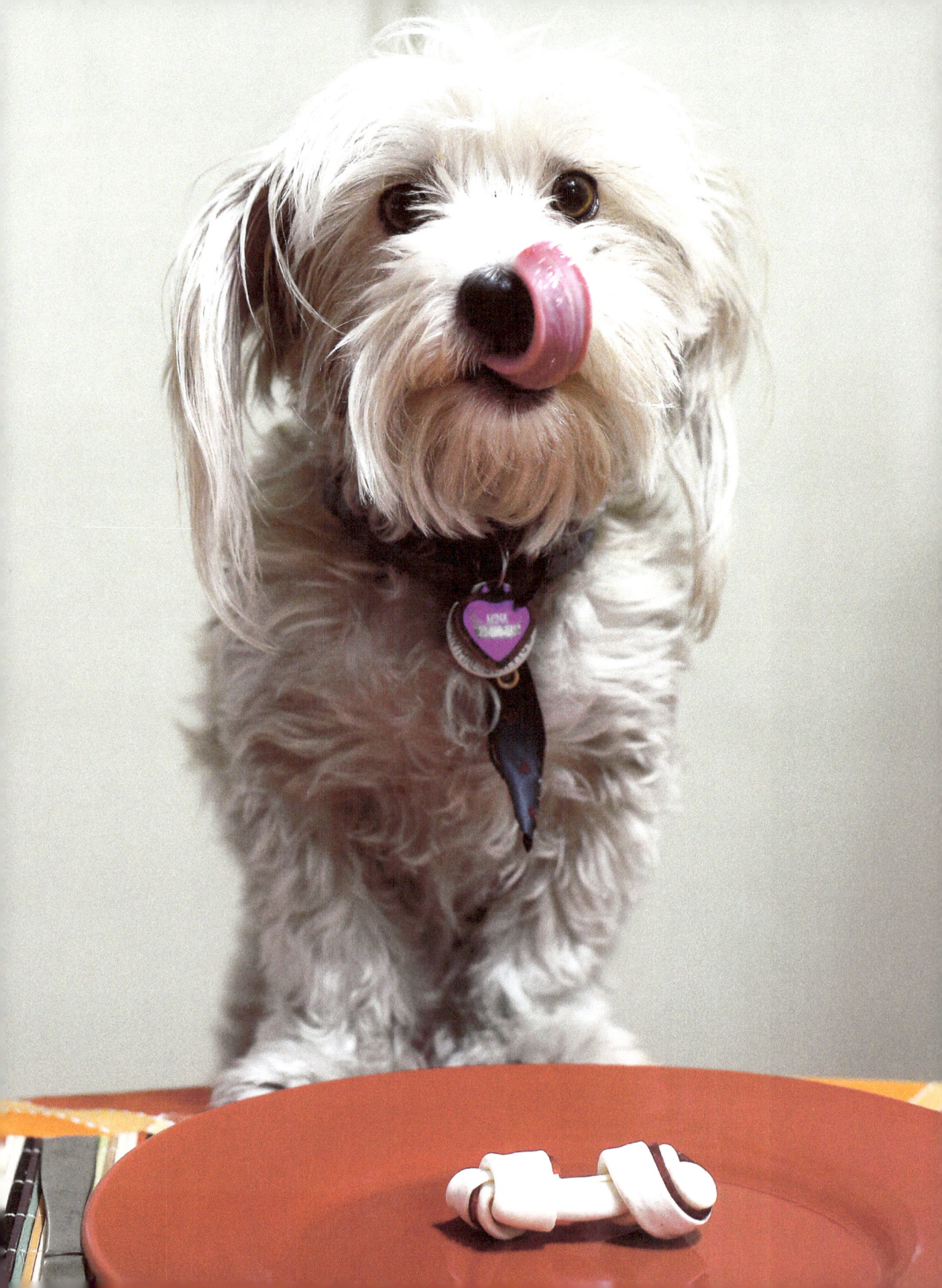

Finally, it is one of my favorite times!

DINNERTIME!!

This bone may look small, but it is gourmet!

"BONE APPETIT!"

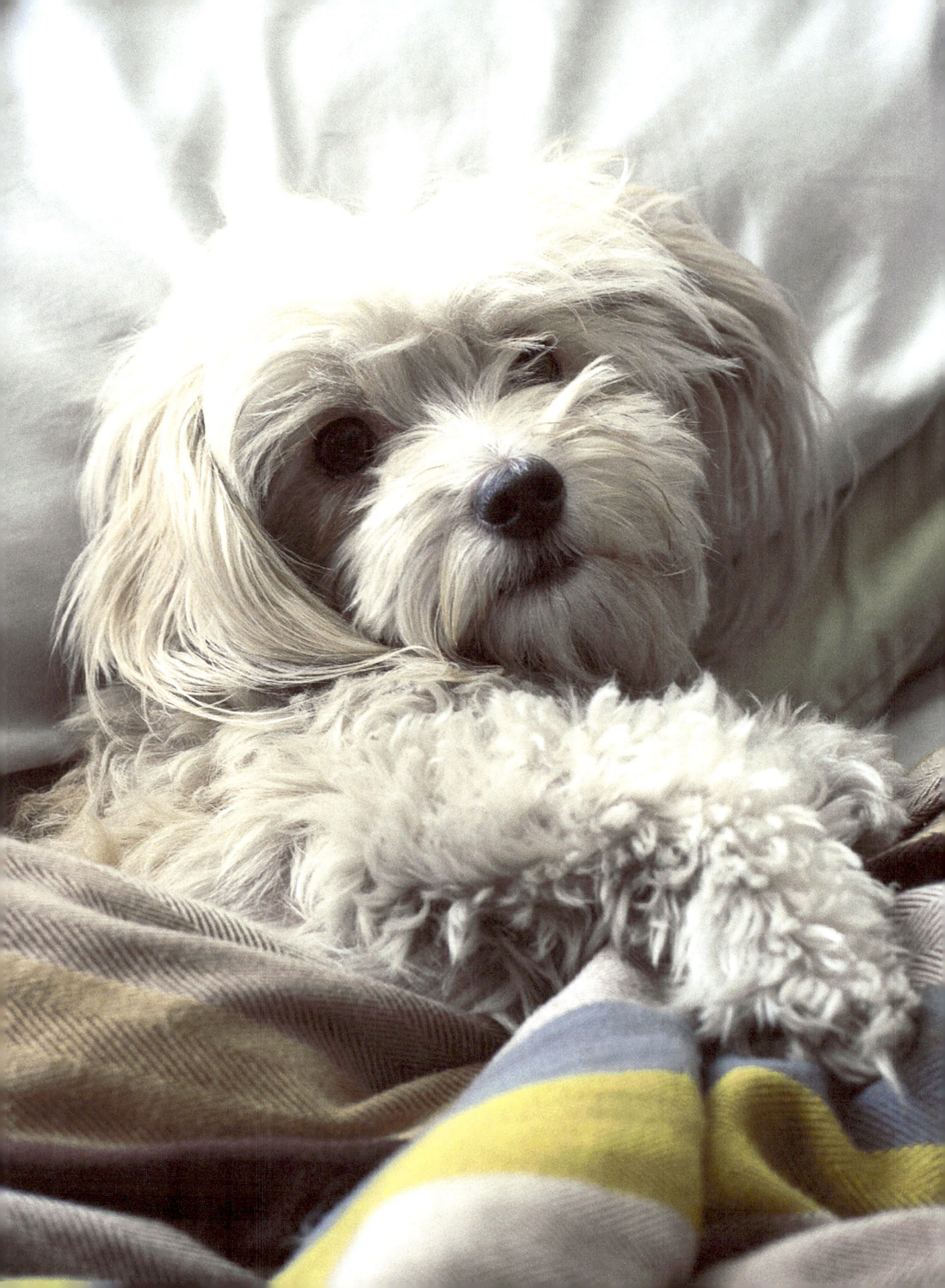

After this very exciting day,

now it is time for bed.

I love to sleep next to my mommy in her bed!

We keep each other warm, and I love to cuddle!

Sweet Dreams!!

May Dog, oops, I mean...

May God bless every creature great and small.

Thank you for sharing a Day in the Life of Mina!

THE END

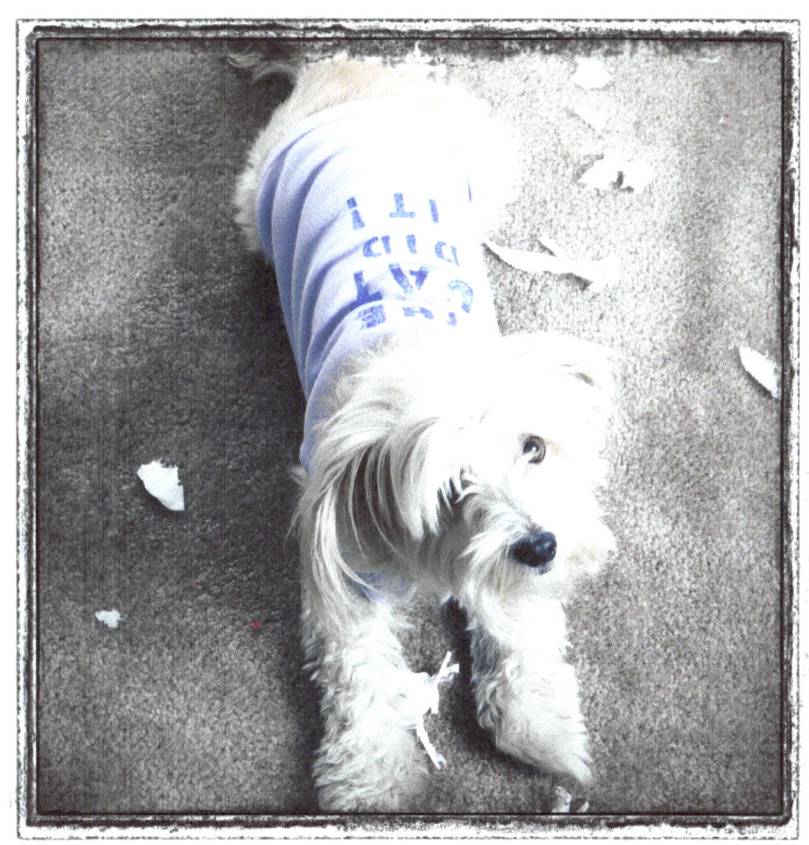

Written by Lauran Doverspike
Photographs by Jeremy Duplaquet

Copyright © 2014

About Jeremy and Lauran

Jeremy and Lauran are neighbors and met each other in Los Angeles

a few years ago. He takes care of Mina sometimes when Lauran

is working, and Mina loves him!

They have decided to make a children's book about Mina, Lauran's Maltese-Mix,

because Mina is very funny and smart, but more importantly,

they felt like sharing a happy story about a rescued dog.

There are so many homeless dogs like Mina who are put to sleep everyday

simply because they are not lucky enough to find homes.

They are hoping that this book will inspire more people to rescue dogs

(and cats) from animal shelters and

experience their unconditional love and friendship.

They always seem to know that you saved them and are eternally grateful and loyal.

Self-published by Jeremy Duplaquet and Lauran Doverspike

jeremyduplaquet@gmail.com

Ldoverspike@yahoo.com

Facebook : Mina TheFree

www.jeremyduplaquet.wordpress.com

www.laurandoverspike.wordpress.com

JD

ISBN-13: 978-0692346884

ISBN-10: 0692346880

BISAC: Pets / Dogs / General